The Book of American Presidents

D1370858

VALDEN MADSEN

With the assistance of
Lucas Alikani Cohen

Mud Puddle Books
NEW YORK

The Book of American Presidents
by Valden Madsen
With the assistance of
Lucas Alikani Cohen

Revised 2nd Printing
Copyright © 2008, 2009 by Mud Puddle Books, Inc.

Published by
Mud Puddle Books, Inc.
54 W. 21st Street
Suite 601
New York, NY 10010
info@mudpuddlebooks.com

ISBN: 978-1-60311-152-2

For complete photographic credits please see page 112.
Photo and caption research by Mulberry Tree Press, Inc.

Interior design and preparation by Mulberry Tree Press, Inc.

Printed in China

★ Contents ★

★ Introduction ★

1. POLITICS, POWER AND THE PRESIDENCY

> "Politics ought to be the part-time profession of every citizen who would
> protect the rights and privileges of free people."
>
> —President Dwight D. Eisenhower, 1954

In this quote, President Eisenhower expresses his belief that political power belongs to the citizens of a free country and that all citizens ought to be involved in the political process. Eisenhower's 1954 phrase "every citizen" meant something different to him than it did to the country's founding fathers. When they began writing the laws for the new country in 1787, they declared, "We the people of the United States." The truth is, however, that they did not include "every citizen" in those days: only white males age 21 and older were allowed to vote. Furthermore, in order to qualify as voters, men usually had to own quite a lot of property. Poorer citizens could not vote. No woman could vote, and that simple fact all by itself cuts the 1787 phrase, "We the people," in half. African-Americans (whether slaves or freedmen) and other people of color (including those who had lived for countless generations on the lands which became the United States) were rarely allowed to vote. With all those restrictions in mind, the 1787 phrase, "We the people of the United States," more accurately becomes, "We, 25% of the people of the United States."

By the time of Dwight Eisenhower's presidency, "every citizen" included far more individuals than "We the people" originally had. The right to vote is basic to a citizen's participation in the political life of his or her nation. Three amendments to the U. S. Constitution since Eisenhower's presidency further expanded the right to vote; each of the three made the definition of "every citizen" even broader. Whenever the right to vote has been enlarged, many people have been fiercely opposed to that expansion. For example, a great many people—almost all white people in the South and a significant number of them in the North—did not want African-Americans to be granted that right in the years following the American Civil War. Women had to fight for close to a half century before they won the right to vote in 1920.

In fact, the right to vote has been one of the battlegrounds between the conservative and the liberal political movements in the United States. Understanding some of the differences between "liberal" and "conservative" helps a person better understand the powers of the presidency and its central role in the political life of the United States.

Generally speaking, the political conservative seeks stability and reliable guides to progress by looking to the past; the liberal seeks progress and reform in the present and future. The conservative believes that government should do less for citizens; the liberal seeks more services from government.

Every one of the forty-four U. S. Presidents can be placed somewhere on the scale stretching between liberal and conservative. For example, Thomas Jefferson, the third President, and Lyndon Johnson, the thirty-sixth, were both liberals. John Adams, the second President, and Ronald Reagan, the thirty-ninth, were examples of conservatives.

In the days of Adams and Jefferson the liberals were called Democratic-Republicans and the conservatives were called Federalists.[1] In modern American history the liberals have traditionally been members of the Democratic party and the conservatives have been Republicans. Obviously, the two political parties have never been composed entirely of either conservatives or liberals. Some modern-day Republicans are more liberal than some Democrats are, and some Democrats are more conservative than some Republicans. A perfect example of such a combination of philosophies is President Eisenhower himself. Although generally thought of as a conservative Republican, he took the radically liberal step in 1957 of using federal troops to enforce court-ordered racial integration in the public schools in Little Rock, Arkansas.

---

[1] The Federalists had pretty well disappeared as a political party by 1816. The Democratic-Republican party dominated American politics from then until the emergence of the Whig

The struggles between the liberal and conservative movements have both created and resolved great American conflicts, beyond determining who has the right to vote. In the process, the nation has moved closer and closer to realizing the democratic ideal President Eisenhower expressed when he used the phrase "every citizen." Three days before he left office on January 20, 1961, Eisenhower spoke about a new danger "every citizen" had to be aware of. He warned against the threat of "the military-industrial complex. The potential for the disastrous rise of misplaced power exists and will persist." The powerful "complex" he spoke of has today become many different special-interest groups. Those groups and their "disastrous rise of misplaced power" dominate the political life of the United States in the Twenty-first Century. This is how it works:

Various industries, including those which supply goods and services to the armed forces of the United States ("the military-industrial complex" itself), hire men and women called lobbyists to represent their interests in conversations with Representatives and Senators.[2] Usually, the lobbyist will offer to contribute money to the politicians' re-election campaigns. Sometimes, but not always, these "contributions" are, in fact, little better than bribes. "If you vote for the special interest I represent," the lobbyist says, "We'll be happy to support your candidacy in the November election."

In recent years, observers of government have noted a further danger to the rights of "every citizen." These days people frequently refer to the "military-industrial-congressional complex." They use Eisenhower's phrase and add the third word to it for this reason: it is now usual for a man or woman to retire from the Congressional or the Executive branch of government and go immediately to work as a lobbyist, representing a special interest group. For example, a former Senator can go directly from serving the people of his state to serving the special

---

party in the late 1830s. There were four Whig Presidents from 1841 through 1853—Harrison, Tyler, Taylor, and Fillmore. These four were not always more conservative than their Democratic-Republican opponents. In the mid-1850s the Whig party disappeared, and the modern Republican party was born. Its first presidential candidate, Abraham Lincoln, was elected in 1860.

[2] Lobbyists earned their name because they used to wait in the lobbies of the Senate or the House of Representatives to speak with politicians. Increasingly, they are seen inside both houses of Congress, doing their work right on the spot, so to speak.

interests of the industry or organization he now lobbies for. His voice carries great weight, obviously, for he was, until recently, a respected colleague of the Senator or Representative whose vote he now seeks for the benefit of the special interest he represents. In the halls of congressional power, such people have considerably more influence than President Eisenhower's "every citizen" ever will. Lobbyists and the groups they represent are anything but democratic.

2. WHO WERE THE PRESIDENTS OF THE UNITED STATES?

Can Eisenhower's "every citizen" hope to become President? That's certainly more a possibility nowadays than it has ever been. So far, however, all have been male and, with the exception of Barack Obama, the forty-four Presidents [3] have all been white. They have come from every walk of life (though a majority of them—twenty-seven—were lawyers before becoming President) and from seventeen of the fifty states. Some were intellectually impressive and some seemed to have been given no great share of brains. Some were highly gifted in foreign affairs, able to form effective alliances with other nations; some were unable to cooperate with anyone. They have been silent or noisy, friendly or withdrawn. A few of them were dishonest and corrupt; most were decent men who did their best under sometimes impossible conditions. Eight of them were born British citizens. Thirteen were born in the 18th Century, twenty in the 19th, and ten in the 20th.

All but one of them (James Buchanan) were married. Five of them had no children, and John Tyler fathered fifteen. Nine of them never attended college (of the thirty-four who did, seven attended Harvard and five went to Yale), and only one of them (Woodrow Wilson) ever earned a Ph.D. A dozen of them were generals in the army before becoming President; many of them never served in the military. Lincoln was the tallest President at 6'4"; James Madison was exactly one foot shorter. Madison was also the lightest President, at less than 100 pounds, while William Howard Taft weighed more than 300. When he was inaugurated in January 1981 at age 69, Ronald Reagan was the oldest man ever elected; John F. Kennedy was the youngest at 43 when he was elected in 1960.

---

[3] There have been forty-three different individuals, but forty-four presidencies. The U.S. Secretary of State ruled that Grover Cleveland's non-consecutive terms (1885–89 and 1893–97) are two different presidencies.

3. THE PRESIDENCY AND THE CONSTITUTION

The United States of America has not always had Presidents nor its present form of government. When the thirteen North American colonies declared their independence from Great Britain in 1776, they joined together in the Continental Congress. The members of the Congress cooperated throughout the Revolutionary War under the Articles of Confederation which established the rules governing the thirteen colonies. The Confederation did not serve the new country well. The individual states had too much power, and there was no central (federal) government that could require citizens or states to pay the taxes that were needed to fight the War for Independence.

After the war ended in 1783, the Continental Congress began to discuss replacing the Articles with something better. Representatives from the colonies met in Philadelphia during the summer of 1787 and put together a set of basic laws called a constitution.

The Constitution was the most complete legal document of its kind in history. Since its adoption by the thirteen United States at the end of the 18th Century, it has been imitated by dozens and dozens of countries. In its original form, the document runs to only about 4,500 words, but it has been proved successful through the 220 years of its existence: it has had to be changed (amended) only 27 times.[4]

The writers of the Constitution (they're usually called "framers" because they built this framework of laws) worked out many compromises. The conservatives

---

[4] The first ten amendments are the Bill of Rights, in which the basic rights of a free people are guaranteed; government may not take any of these rights away from citizens without giving very good reasons. Among these rights are freedom of speech and freedom of (and from) religion; a citizen accused of a crime has the right to a speedy and fair trial; no officer of the law may enter a citizen's home (or read his or her mail or e-mail) without first having a very strong reason and then obtaining a court's permission to do so. Truth to tell, these ten aren't "amendments" in the sense that the other seventeen are, since they are absolutely fundamental to what is best in the Constitution and in the United States. Members of the Constitutional Convention knew that the Bill of Rights would be included in the Constitution: the Bill was approved by the states in 1791, only three years after the Constitution itself was adopted by the states. Among the other seventeen amendments, the Twenty-first (1933) repealed (canceled) the Eighteenth (1919), the amendment forbidding the manufacture and sale of alcoholic beverages in the United States.

wanted one kind of institution, the liberals wanted another. Time and time again George Washington himself was called upon to mediate between the two political movements. For example, Jefferson was deeply disturbed by the way his conservative colleagues wanted to form the legislative branch. How can we pretend to be democratic, he wondered, when the tiny state of Delaware will have as many senators as the huge state of Pennsylvania will have?

As president of the Convention, Washington sat down with Jefferson many times to win the younger man over to the conservative point of view. Washington finally convinced him to accept the non-democratic political reality the constitution still expresses: every state is represented by two senators, no matter the size of its population. Membership in the House of Representatives is based on the population of the individual states. Thus, large states such as California (53 representatives), Texas (32) and New York (29) all have two senators each, as do states small in population such as Montana, Vermont, and North Dakota. Very small states such as these (there are actually seven of them) have only one representative each.[5]

After all the arguing and compromising, the Constitution was written to accomplish two great goals: first, it had to lay out the rights and responsibilities of a free people in a democratic republic, a country not controlled by a king or queen. A republic, however, is not a pure democracy. The best example of a pure democracy is an old-fashioned New England town meeting in which citizens cast their votes directly for or against a question facing the community. In a republic, elected individuals make the legal decisions for the people they represent. The second goal of the Constitution of the United States was to express what has come to be known as the separation of powers.

4. THE CONSTITUTION DEFINES THREE BRANCHES OF GOVERNMENT

The framers of the Constitution knew that they wanted to lay out the rules for a democratic republic. Beyond that simple beginning, they were in unexplored territory. They had very few existing governments to model their efforts

---

[5] The other four are Alaska, Delaware, South Dakota, and Wyoming. Since a law passed in 1911, the number of representatives has been fixed at 435. The number of a state's representatives rises or falls as states gain or lose population.

on. European and Asian nations were almost all governed by kings, queens, emperors, or other tyrannical rulers. Democratic principles in Europe started with the French Revolution, which did not begin until two years after the American Constitution was written.

The framers knew that they wanted a government that would respond to the needs of the people. They also wanted to be sure that they were creating a government which could not overpower its own citizens. To this end they determined that the federal government should be separated into three branches: the judicial, the legislative, and the executive.

According to the Constitution, each branch has its own powers and responsibilities. The Supreme Court of the United States and all lesser federal courts make up the judicial branch; the Congress, made up of the House of Representatives and the Senate, is the legislative branch; and the executive is the Presidency. Only the third branch of government, the executive, is just one person. (In contrast, there are 100 senators and 435 representatives in the legislative branch.)

Because the executive is one individual, the framers were careful not to create an executive authority who could easily abuse presidential powers. The framers did not want to create an American king. In fact, when some members of the Constitutional Convention wanted to have George Washington declared King of the United States of America, the great General himself closed the subject with a definite "no."

The three separate branches of government are equal to one another, and are intended to balance each other. In this way, they act as brakes, or checks, on each other's powers.

The Constitution says simply that "The executive Power shall be vested in a President of the United States." The fact that the executive power should be confined to one individual was not obvious to all the framers. Some of them wanted a plural executive, a kind of executive committee to take on the responsibilities of the office. This model often works well in business—a Board of Directors presided over by its Chairperson—but wiser heads prevailed at the Constitutional Convention. The institution of the unitary (single) executive was written into constitutional law. Even the choice of the title, "President," took some doing. Some people wanted a more dignified word, something on the order of "His Highness" or "His Majesty" (some of the titles given to the

British King) but Washington thought "President" was more democratic. Also, he was already the president of the Constitutional Convention, and no one doubted that he would be the country's first President.

5. WHO CAN BE PRESIDENT OF THE UNITED STATES?

It was easier for the framers to agree on what the President's qualifications were than on how he was to be elected.[6] They decided that the President had to be at least thirty-five years old and a natural born citizen of the U.S. or a citizen of the country at the time the Constitution was adopted; he would receive a salary—the $25,000 annual salary refused by George Washington rose to $400,000 by the time the Forty-third President, George W. Bush, took office. The constitutional oath of office does not mention religion or God:

> "I do solemnly swear (or affirm) that I will faithfully execute the Office of President of the United States, and will to the best of my Ability, preserve, protect and defend the Constitution of the United States."

All Presidents have added the words, "So help me God," though the phrase is not required.

6. HOW IS THE PRESIDENT NOT ELECTED?

The "how" of presidential elections fills several books. The framers had a number of options. Any one of them had to take into account the facts of life in the United States of 1787. The country had only about 4,000,000 people, and its thirteen states were spread out along the Atlantic coast from New Hampshire

---

[6] The constitution as originally written says almost nothing about who has the right to vote for President or for any other officeholder. The framers left the question of voter qualifications up to the individual states. Most states required that a voter be a white male, aged 21 or older, who owned property or paid taxes. During the first years of the 19th Century, property requirements gradually disappeared. Later in the country's history, five amendments to the Constitution expanded the right to vote: the Fifteenth (1870) guaranteed voting rights to racial minorities; the Nineteenth (1920) to women; the Twenty-third (1961) allowed citizens of the District of Columbia to vote in presidential elections; the Twenty-fourth (1964) denied any state the power to impose a special tax on voters (the poll tax); eighteen to twenty-year-olds were granted the right to vote by the Twenty-sixth amendment in 1971.

in the north to Georgia in the south. There were no phones, no faxes, no radio, no television, no internet. The fastest way to get the news from one place to another was to put a man on a horse and send him galloping off. If something important happened in Boston, people in Philadelphia wouldn't hear about it until the following week or even month. The framers of the constitution had to keep the geographical facts of life in mind. In creating the office of the President, they also needed to maintain the balance of power between the states and the federal government. Equally important, they had to ensure the balance of power between the executive and legislative branches within the federal government.

To make the situation even more complicated, there were no political parties back then. The framers believed such groups were evil. Although there have always been liberal and conservative political movements in American politics, parties as they are known today did not come into existence until several years after the Constitution was created. Finally, and this seems unbelievable today when we seem to live in a world of endless political campaigning, men who ran for office did not campaign in those days. It was said that the office went in search of the man, not the reverse.

So, once the framers determined that we needed an executive branch headed by a President who'd be the most powerful person in our government, they asked themselves, how do we go about electing him? They first thought that the state legislatures might elect the President but decided that that would give too much power to the states. (State legislatures did appoint U. S. Senators until the Seventeenth Amendment to the Constitution gave that power directly to voters in 1913.) Next they considered allowing Congress to vote a President into office, but that idea died as soon as it was born: that would have destroyed the balance of power between the legislative and the executive branches. A third possibility was the direct election of the President by the voters. That would not have worked because, as noted above, the population was so spread out and communication among parts of the country was so slow that people in one part of the country wouldn't know anything about candidates from any other part.

7. THE ELECTORAL COLLEGE ELECTS THE PRESIDENT

The fourth possibility was adopted by the Constitutional Convention and provides that the President shall be elected by an Electoral College. The term

"Electoral College" never actually appears in the Constitution, though the word "electors" is used in Article II and again in the Twelfth amendment. The framers borrowed the concept of the Electoral College from the government of the Holy Roman Empire, which dominated central Europe for nearly nine hundred years, from the Tenth to the Nineteenth centuries. In that system the electors were princes who met to elect an emperor. In addition to the Holy Roman Empire, the founders found another such college of electors in history, one which still exists: the Roman Catholic College of Cardinals elects the new pope whenever an old one dies.

This is how our Electoral College works, according to the U.S. Constitution. Each state is assigned Electors equal to its number of representatives plus its two senators. A state with seven members in the House of Representatives, therefore, can cast nine votes in the Electoral College. When an individual voter casts a ballot for John Roe or Jane Doe in a presidential election, the vote actually goes to that candidate's Electors. Although modified in important ways, the Electoral College still elects the President of the United States, meeting in December following the November presidential election once every four years.

Although the Electors should obviously vote according to the results of the popular vote in their states, neither the Constitution nor any federal law requires them to do so. However, many individual states have laws that require Electors to obey the popular vote. In theory, an Elector from a state without such a law could vote for anyone he or she chose to vote for. Pushed to the limit, this theory would make quite a movie: a group of rogue Electors decide that they will disobey the popular vote in their individual states and vote into office a President of their own choosing. No federal law would forbid this outcome. In the real world, however, the Electors have obeyed the will of the people and have voted in accordance with the popular vote more than 99% of the time.

Almost all of the fifty states assign their electoral votes on a winner-take-all basis. If the popular vote in a given state divides 49.9% to 50.1%, the candidate who wins by two-tenths of one percent wins all the electoral votes of that state. This strikes many people as undemocratic, and from time to time there are movements which seek to assign electoral votes according to the popular vote. Thus, using the example given above, based on a state with 25 electoral votes, the winner would be given 13 votes and the loser 12.

As originally described in the Constitution, the Electoral College voted as follows: the candidate with the most votes became President, and the one who came in second served as his Vice President. Almost immediately, this practice became problematic. In 1796 John Adams was elected President by one electoral vote, 71-70, over Thomas Jefferson, his most bitter political enemy. Jefferson therefore became Vice President, which meant that Adams's second-in-command was his worst enemy for four difficult years. It was like asking a tiger to live with a lion.

Four years later, in the election of 1800, the crisis came: none of the leading candidates for President achieved a majority of Electoral votes. Jefferson and Aaron Burr each won 73 votes, John Adams won 65 and Charles Pinckney 64. Thus, according to the Constitution, the election went to the House of Representatives where each state was given one vote. After an extended political battle which nearly destroyed the young nation, Thomas Jefferson was elected on the 36th ballot.

Congress immediately set out to amend the Constitution in an effort to simplify the election process. The Twelfth amendment to the Constitution (1804) directs that the Electors will cast separate ballots for President and for Vice President. Since 1804, a President and his Vice President have always run for office on the same ticket; it has been clearly understood that they are not in competition for the Presidency. In case no candidate for President wins a majority of Electoral ballots, the House will choose from among the top three individuals, not from among the top five, as originally written. In addition to the election of 1800, the House has performed this constitutional duty only in 1824, when it elected John Quincy Adams over Andrew Jackson. Jackson had won the popular vote but neither Adams nor he had won a majority of the Electoral votes.

8. SHOULD AMERICA DO AWAY WITH THE ELECTORAL COLLEGE?

Most Americans (between 58% and 81%, depending upon the poll and the year) believe that the Electoral College should no longer be used. Now that the mass media make politicians' faces and ideas familiar to all voters everywhere, the College fulfills no positive function. Former Senator Robert Dole, the Republican candidate for President in 1996, believes the College gives states with smaller populations a voice in electing Presidents. In fact, though, that voice is neither democratic nor fair. One could say that voters in small states have louder voices than citizens of large states do. The state of Wyoming, with 509,000 people, has three electoral votes, or about one vote per 170,000 residents. The 36,000,000 residents of California have 55 electoral votes, or about one per 655,000 citizens. If California were given electoral votes on the Wyoming model, Californians would have about 212. Put another way, the Wyomingite has nearly four times the voting power of a Californian.

On the other hand, Senator Dole has a point. There are a total of 538 electoral votes, 535 from the fifty states and three from the District of Columbia. The eleven largest states have 271 votes, one more than necessary to elect a President. Theoretically, the votes of the other 39 states might not count. In the real world, however, that wouldn't happen, since the eleven include both traditionally liberal (for example, New York and California) and traditionally conservative (North Carolina and Texas, for example) states.

The Electoral College can actually defeat the democratic process when a candidate wins the popular vote but loses the Electoral vote. This happened in 1824, 1876, 1888, and, most recently, in the 2000 election between Republican Governor George W. Bush and Democratic Vice President Al Gore. An extended legal argument in Florida was finally settled by a 5–4 decision of the Supreme Court which gave Florida's 27 Electoral votes to Mr. Bush. Thus he won with 271 Electoral votes to 266 for Mr. Gore. A messy recount revealed that Bush had won that state by just 537 votes out of more than six million cast. Nationally, however, Gore won the popular vote by 48.38% to Bush's 47.87%, a little more than half of one percent (.51%). A useful historical contrast is the 1960 presidential election in which John F. Kennedy bested Richard Nixon by less than half that amount (.20%) and became the nation's Thirty-fifth President.[7]

---

[7] Very rarely does a president win more than 60% of the popular vote. Warren Harding won 60.3% in 1920; Franklin Roosevelt 60.8% in 1936; Lyndon Johnson 61.1%, the greatest majority ever, in 1964; Richard Nixon won 60.7% in 1972. Winning more than 55% of

Most Americans believe that they should be able to elect their Presidents by direct vote. The Electoral College unfairly weights the votes of small states. Moreover, citizens of the United States should never again have to risk the consequences of the undemocratic election of 2000.

9. Constitutional Amendments and the Presidency

If proposed and passed, a constitutional amendment removing the Electoral Collage would be the fifth dealing directly with the presidency. The Twelfth amendment (1804), previously noted, was the first. The second was the Twentieth (1933) which changed Inauguration Day from March 4 to January 20 and outlined the role of an acting president. The third "presidential amendment" was the Twenty-second (1951), which limited the President to two terms. (Only Franklin Roosevelt had ever been elected to more than two terms: he was elected in 1932, 1936, 1940 and 1944.) In 1967 the Twenty-fifth amendment laid out the rules governing the presidential succession.

Section 1 of that amendment puts in writing what had always been done: the Vice President succeeds to the presidency when the President dies in office or resigns (in 1967 no President had yet resigned). Section 2 orders that, when there is no Vice President, the President nominates a candidate who must be confirmed by both houses of the Congress. This happened in 1973 when Richard Nixon's first Vice President, Spiro Agnew, resigned. Nixon nominated Gerald Ford, who became President when Nixon himself resigned in 1974. In his turn, Ford nominated Nelson Rockefeller as Vice President. Rockefeller was confirmed by the Congress in December of 1974. For 25 months, from then until January 20, 1977, when Jimmy Carter was inaugurated, the United States had both a President and a Vice President for whom not a single citizen had voted.

Section 3 orders that the President temporarily give his powers to the Vice President (who then becomes the Acting President) when he is unable to discharge them. The President routinely does this when he undergoes surgery or

the popular vote means election by a landslide in recent American history. The following victories are much more representative: John F. Kennedy in 1960 with 49.7%, Richard Nixon in 1968 with 43.4% (a third-party candidate that year won 13.5% of the vote), Jimmy Carter in 1976 with 50.1%, Bill Clinton in 1992 with 43.3% (a third-party candidate won 19%), and George W. Bush in 2004 with 50.7%.

must be anesthetized for another medical procedure. Section 4 of the amendment is long and complicated. In it are detailed the ways in which a President may be removed from office by other members of the government, from both the executive and legislative branches. The Section also outlines the legal ways in which the President can object to such removal.

10. HOW CAN A PRESIDENT BE REMOVED FROM OFFICE?

Apart from Section 4 of the 25th Amendment to the Constitution, the President can be removed from office only through impeachment. An ordinary citizen who is suspected of breaking the law is charged in a regular court, but Presidents, Vice Presidents and other high officers of government must be impeached rather than charged. To set the process in motion, the Judiciary Committee of the House of Representatives draws up charges against the President. These charges are called "articles of impeachment." If the Judiciary Committee agrees to impeach the President, the whole House of Representatives votes on the matter. If a majority of the Representatives in the House agrees with the Committee, it is said that the President is impeached.

The process next moves to the U. S. Senate. The 100 senators hear evidence from Representatives who either accuse or defend the President. The Chief Justice of the United States, the highest legal officer in the country, is in charge of the proceedings. If a majority of the Senators finds the President guilty of "Treason, Bribery, or other high Crimes and Misdemeanors," (to quote the Constitution) he is removed from office and is automatically replaced by the Vice President.

The impeachment of a President is a very serious matter. Almost always, the members of Congress will try to avoid it and seek other ways of working with or against a President. No matter how much a Representative or Senator may hate a President, or disagree with his policies or behavior, most reasonable people agree that impeachment is a tragic last resort. In fact, in the 220 years since the Constitution was adopted, only three Presidents have been subjected to the impeachment process.

Andrew Johnson was impeached by the House but not convicted by the Senate in 1868. In 1998 Bill Clinton was also impeached but not convicted. Richard Nixon would certainly have been both impeached by the House and convicted by the Senate had he not resigned in August, 1974, before the whole House could vote. Some people believe that officials should be impeached more often, though most disagree.

11. How does the Constitution describe the President's job?

The President's constitutional duties are hugely demanding. Most Presidents work very long days, take few vacations and age several years for each year they spend in office.

First of all, the President is the Commander-in-Chief of all the armed forces of the United States. The framers of the Constitution were very proud of this important detail: they placed the armed forces under civilian control, not under the control of a general or admiral or other military officer. Americans need never worry that some powerful general is going to go berserk, take over the armed forces and declare war on another country. Sometimes military leaders may grumble or complain, but there is never any question that the final authority and responsibility for military decisions come from the White House. In a nation of 300 million citizens with an Alaska-sized military budget, being Commander-in-Chief means a lot of work.

Presidents of the United States are also responsible for preparing and presenting the federal budget to the Congress. Members of the legislative branch then modify his proposals. The President has the power to veto (to say no to) any suggestion or change he does not agree with. The federal budget for the twelve months beginning in October, 2008 amounts to approximately $3,100,000,000,000 (three trillion, one hundred billion dollars).

The President can grant pardons, which means that the person being pardoned can't be legally punished for any crime or wrongdoing. The President can pardon anyone for any offense or crime whatsoever, "except in Cases of Impeachment," the Constitution says. Obviously, if a President is being impeached, it wouldn't be a good idea for him to be able to pardon himself! This great privilege is rarely used by Presidents; to overuse it would be an abuse of presidential power. The most unpopular pardon in anyone's memory was probably President Ford's pardon of former President Nixon in the fall of 1974, following Nixon's resignation of the presidency. President Ford defended his action, saying that it was necessary for the country to move beyond the painful facts of President Nixon's criminal behavior.

With the "advice and consent of the Senate," to quote the Constitution, the President can make treaties with other nations, appoint ambassadors and nominate judges to the Supreme Court and other federal courts. Because this judicial power of the presidency is so great, the framers of the Constitution made sure that no judge could be appointed without two-thirds of the senators agreeing.

The Constitution also requires that the President "shall from time to time give to the Congress Information of the State of the Union." This has become the annual "State of the Union Address" each President gives every January. In modern times it has become quite a media event, with much attention being paid to who's been invited and who sits where. All Representatives and Senators, as well as members of the Supreme Court and the invited public, gather in the Capitol building to hear the President's speech. Not in attendance on that important night is at least one member of the President's cabinet (his inner circle of advisers): he or she would become the next President if the Capitol building were blown up and there were no other survivors. There must be someone left alive to succeed to the Presidency under the terms of the Presidential Succession law of 1947.[8]

The President works with the Congress to create laws, and also has the power to call one or both houses of Congress into session. The Congress writes laws (temporarily called "bills") which are then sent to the President. If he signs a bill, it becomes a law. If he disagrees with its content and either refuses to sign it or vetoes it, one of two things happens to the bill: 1) it never becomes law or 2) two-thirds of the Senators and Representatives defy the President and vote against his wishes. The bill then becomes a law without the presidential signature. In effect, this means that one person, the President, has more power than 65 Senators (one fewer than two-thirds of the Senate) and 289 Representatives (one fewer than two-thirds of the House). Let no one ever doubt the power of the President of the United States.

---

[8] President Harry S. Truman signed this Act into law. It provides for the presidential succession in the event that both the President and the Vice President are killed or if both of them are unable to serve. In that case, the Speaker of the House of Representatives would become President. If he or she is unavailable or incapable, then the office goes to the Secretary of State, then to the Secretary of Defense and so on down through the cabinet Secretaries, in the order in which their specific Departments were created, ending up with number eighteen, the Secretary of Homeland Security, a Department created by law in 2002 and established in 2003.

12. THE PRESIDENT HAS POWERS NOT LISTED IN THE CONSTITUTION

In addition to the President's constitutional powers, the years have added other powers to the office. President Truman said that the office shrinks or expands to fit the person sitting in it. As an example, Mr. Truman pointed to the eight relatively weak Presidents who served from the time of Andrew Jackson (he left office in 1837) up until Abraham Lincoln came to Washington in 1861. During those twenty-four years the office of the presidency shrank, and Congress was the more powerful branch of government.

The presidency always grows more powerful during wartime. This has been true from the Civil War to the 21st Century's War on Terror. As President Lincoln (1861–1865) denied many American citizens basic civil and legal rights, so did President George W. Bush (2001–2009) take away some of those same rights. Franklin Delano Roosevelt (1933–1945) allowed Japanese-Americans living on the West Coast to be taken from their homes and businesses and detained in camps during the Second World War. Referring to this abuse of power, Roosevelt's chief legal adviser (Attorney General Francis Biddle) simply observed that, "The Constitution has never greatly bothered any wartime president."

American citizens of Japanese descent had done nothing wrong; they were discriminated against because of their racial heritage. Because the United States was at war with Japan at the time, President Roosevelt had no trouble denying more than 120,000 Japanese-Americans access to their Constitution's Bill of Rights.

When Congress is controlled by members of the President's own political party, presidential power expands especially rapidly in time of war. This was true with reference to Lincoln and Roosevelt and was also true in George W. Bush's case from 2001 until 2007. At its extreme, the power of the President can seem almost equal to that of a Roman emperor's. Indeed, the famous historian, Arthur M. Schlesinger, Jr., titled his 1973 study of the subject *The Imperial Presidency*.

Professor Schlesinger argues that the U. S. presidency began to outgrow its constitutional description during the Depression and wartime presidency of Franklin Roosevelt. Politically liberal, Roosevelt used the power of his office in ways that no President had before. The power of the presidency has continued to grow in the decades since Roosevelt's death in 1945. It goes without saying that no President, whether liberal or conservative, ever gives up power willingly.

No matter who the President has been, the powers of the office have increased. Human nature almost never wants to shrink.

In the past thirty years, presidential power has increased dramatically through Presidents' use of what is called the "signing statement." What does this phrase mean? When a President signs a bill into law, he may issue an accompanying statement saying he will interpret and enforce that law "in a manner consistent with my constitutional authority to supervise the unitary executive branch." (The idea of "unitary executive" is discussed in Section 4, The Constitution Defines Three Branches of Government.)

In the 164 years from the presidency of James Monroe (1817–1825) through that of Jimmy Carter (1977–1981), Presidents issued such statements a total of just 75 times. The three Presidents who served for the twenty years between 1981 and 2001 (Reagan, George H. W. Bush and Clinton) issued a total of 322 signing statements, about 16 per year. In his first term, 2001-2005, George W. Bush issued approximately 125 such statements, more than 30 per year. His enthusiastic use of the "signing statement" continued in his second term.

As noted above, wartime Presidents usually have more power than peacetime Presidents do. The first presidency of the 21st Century was no exception to that rule. Three days after the terrorist attacks on September 11, 2001, the Congress of the United States hurriedly passed the War Powers Resolution and a Joint Resolution. These two Resolutions passed 98–0 in the Senate and in the House of Representatives by a vote of 420–1. They gave the President of the United States almost unlimited power to wage war against countries guilty of or suspected of terrorist acts or of providing safe places for terrorists.

A month later, in October of 2001, Congress passed the USA PATRIOT Act,[9] which gives the federal government free access to citizens' tax and medical records and allows officers of the law to keep track of citizens' rentals and purchases of books and movies. Moreover, under the terms of the Act, law enforcement personnel may even enter citizens' homes secretly, without having to give any reason for doing so. Since 2001, many cases involving such actions on the

---

[9] The initials of the Act stand for: Uniting and Strengthening America by Providing Appropriate Tools Required to Intercept and Obstruct Terrorism. Only Russell Feingold of Wisconsin voted against the Act in the Senate. When the Act came up for renewal in 2005, nine

part of the police have been brought to court. The judicial branch of government has most often disagreed with the actions of the executive branch in these cases. Judges have usually ordered that no one, including the President's own officials from the Department of Justice, may interfere with a citizen's constitutional freedoms as listed in the Bill of Rights.

Thus the judicial branch of government has reduced the powers given to the President by the Congress in the Resolutions of 2001 and in the PATRIOT Act. This is how the constitutional separation of powers is supposed to work. If one of the three branches of government grows too powerful, it is up to one or both of the others to reduce that power. Even though the courts and Congress have begun to reclaim power, it is no exaggeration to say that the President in office in 2008 had powers unequalled in the 220-year history of the Executive branch.

Some legal scholars believe that a President of the United States must have all this power in order to do the best job possible in times of war. Others believe the opposite point of view: that no President has the right to declare war,[10] no right to suppress civil liberties, no license to set aside any elements of the Constitution's Bill of Rights.

In this, as in all questions regarding the behavior of the federal government and the rights of citizens in a democratic republic, the Constitution is the final authority. That document draws a distinct line between the power of Congress and the power of the President. This "separation of powers" is one of the guiding principles of the Constitution. The words of the Constitution are clear: Congress shall "make all laws" and the President shall "take care that the laws be faithfully executed."

Many experts who study the workings of government believe that recent Presidents have gone well beyond their constitutional limitations. They argue that presidential "signing statements" actually mean that Presidents may execute (enforce) the laws only as they interpret them. They can ignore the inten-

---

senators joined with Senator Feingold in voting against it. In the House, the 2001 vote in favor of the Act was 357-66. The 2005 renewal of the Act was approved by a much narrower margin, 251-174 votes.

[10] Article 1, Section 8 of the Constitution reserves this right to Congress. Woodrow Wilson and Franklin Roosevelt both asked Congress to undertake this action before entering into World Wars I and II.

tion of congress and avoid the rulings of the Supreme Court itself.[11] In some views, a President who ignores the will of Congress has committed impeachable offenses. At the minimum, if Senators and Representatives believe that the Executive has begun taking power which rightfully belongs to the Congress, then members of the House and Senate must reclaim that power.

13. THE PRESIDENT AS A SYMBOLIC FIGURE

In addition to all his—or her—powers, the U.S. President is also an important symbolic figure in America. One has only to watch the inaugural festivities in Washington, D. C. on the 20th of January every fourth year to appreciate the value the country attaches to the presidency. The Chief Justice of the United States administers the oath of office to the new President while the outgoing President looks on. Americans are proud that this ceremony has gone on undisturbed through the centuries.

The President is both head of state and head of government. This is in contrast with, for example, Britain where Queen Elizabeth is head of state and her prime minister is head of government. The President formally greets foreign leaders and travels the world as an unofficial ambassador. His speeches to the United Nations are always cause for media coverage.

As the single most important person in the country, the President is often called upon to inspire the people in times of crisis. Abraham Lincoln did this in his proclamation of a national Thanksgiving Day in 1863, in the midst of Civil War; Franklin Roosevelt calmly and regularly spoke to his fellow Americans in person or on the radio during the twin crises of the Great Depression and the Second World War; George W. Bush delivered a message of hope to his countrymen on the national day of mourning following the terrorist attacks on the eleventh of September, 2001.

---

[11] In July, 2006 a Task Force of the American Bar Association (the professional organization of America's lawyers) determined that such presidential expression of constitutional authority will "undermine the rule of law and our constitutional system of separation of powers."

The White House is where the President lives and works. The site was selected by Pierre Charles L'Enfant, the man who planned the city of Washington. A competition was held to select an architect and nine designs were submitted. James Hoban, the winner, was chosen by George Washington. The cornerstone was laid in 1792 and construction took eight years. President John Adams took up residence on November 1, 1800. During the War of 1812 the White House was burned by the British. It was completely rebuilt and expanded. Expansion, reconstruction and structural maintenance continued off-and-on until 1952. The interior was extensively redecorated with an eye for historic accuracy by First Lady Jacqueline Kennedy (1961–63).

The mandate creating the American flag was adopted by the Second Continental Congress on June 14, 1777 in Philadelphia. It read:

> Resolved, that the flag of the United States be thirteen stripes, alternate red and white; that the union be thirteen stars, white in a blue field representing a new constellation.

The name of the designer of the flag has been lost to history, but many historians believe it to be Francis Hopkinson, a Congressman from New Jersey and signer of the Declaration of Independence. Among a number of early flag makers, Betsy Ross of Philadelphia was the most well-known. In fact, she made flags for more than 50 years. Her flag (*pictured above, left*) with the stars placed in a circle appeared in the early 1790s.

With each addition to the Union, the stars were increased. Today's flag (*above, right*) was the result of an Executive Order by President Eisenhower in 1959, marking the addition of Hawaii and Alaska to the United States.

The flag is known sometimes as The Stars and Stripes and sometimes as "Old Glory." The name "Old Glory" comes from a Massachusetts sea captain, William Driver. Hoisting a flag as he set sail in 1831, he exclaimed as he watched the flag billowing in the breeze, "Old Glory." For the rest of his life, he carried this flag with him.

George Washington
(1732–1799)

★ **First President, 1789–1797** ★

GEORGE WASHINGTON is the most famous American, even though he lived the first two-thirds of his life as a faithful subject of the King of England. Everyone knows who Washington was, and no one can spend a dollar bill without seeing his portrait. He is the "Father of his Country." However, he never wanted to be famous. He was much happier at Mount Vernon, his plantation in Virginia, than he was serving as Commander-in-Chief of American troops during the Revolutionary War (1775–1781). After the thirteen American colonies won their freedom from Great Britain, Washington wanted to retire to his beloved Mount Vernon.

His new country needed him, though, so he

First Lady, Martha Dandridge Custis Washington, 1731–1802.

Washington crossing the Delaware on December 25, 1776, during the American Revolutionary War. The heroic crossing began the surprise attack against the Hessians, German soldiers hired by the King of England, in the Battle of Trenton, New Jersey.

went to Philadelphia in 1787. That summer, representatives of the thirteen states wrote the federal constitution. This is the highest legal authority of the United States. It guarantees the rights of citizens and limits the powers of government. Without Washington's high reputation and personal influence, there would have been no constitution. As president of the convention, he was able to persuade its members to work together. Without a constitution, there would have been no United States. When the new constitution was accepted by the states, the Electoral College gave every one of its votes to George Washington as the first President. Washington is perhaps the only man who could have successfully served as the first President. Politicians and ordinary citizens all thought very highly of him. Even those who disagreed with his policies listened respectfully to him. When he died, less than three years after leaving office, the whole country mourned his death.

George Washington and the Marquis de Lafayette with Washington's family on the lawn of his beloved home, Mount Vernon, near Alexandria, Virginia.

John Adams
(1735–1826)

★ **Second President, 1797–1801** ★

JOHN ADAMS was not happy as George Washington's Vice President. Adams had been active in the movement for American independence from its beginnings in the 1760s. In contrast to all his important work during the Revolutionary War and at the Constitutional Convention, being Vice President was a disappointment. In a letter to his wife, Abigail, he described the vice-presidency as a "most insignificant office."

First Lady, Abigail Smith Adams, 1744–1818.

He was elected President after Washington's retirement. As the constitution was then written, the person who won the second highest number of electoral votes became Vice President. In the election of 1796 that was Thomas Jefferson. However, Adams and Jefferson violently disagreed about political matters. Jefferson's friends in the House and Senate, as well as in the newspapers, made Adams's life miserable. In 1798 Adams and his allies in Congress passed the Alien and Sedition Acts. These laws frightened Adams's political enemies into silence. If a newspaper published a story attacking the President, the Acts allowed the police to close that newspaper down. This was one of the first abuses of Presidential power in U.S. history. Adams retired to his farm in Quincy, Massachusetts after the election of 1800. He and Thomas Jefferson later became close friends. They both died on the Fourth of July, 1826.

Benjamin Franklin, John Adams and Thomas Jefferson, meet at Jefferson's lodgings, on the corner of Seventh and High (Market) streets in Philadelphia, to review a draft of the Declaration of Independence.

In 1934 a commemorative 2-cent stamp was issued by the U.S. Postal Service honoring John Adams.

Thomas Jefferson
(1743–1826)

★ **Third President, 1801–1809** ★

O N APRIL 29, 1962 President John F. Kennedy hosted a dinner for Nobel Prize winners. In his complimentary greetings, he said, "I think this is the most extraordinary collection of talent, of human knowledge, that has ever been gathered together at the White House—with the possible exception of when Thomas Jefferson dined alone." Kennedy was not far off the mark. Jefferson was a scientist and a philosopher, a farmer and a theologian, a politician and an inventor. He was intelligent and well-read, a man devoted to the life of the mind. He had always been a supporter of American nationhood. He wrote the Declara-

Jefferson holding the Declaration of Independence.

tion of Independence in 1776. He was one of the most influential members of the Constitutional Convention of 1787. Working with others, he helped determine the rights and privileges of individuals and states. He served in the administrations of both Washington and Adams, the two men who preceded him in the presidency. With his election in 1800 the system of

The Louisiana Purchase Treaty made official Jefferson's purchase of almost 525 million acres of land in the Mississippi valley from Napoleon of France. Napoleon needed the money, and Jefferson got a good deal at about 3.5 cents per acre.

political parties in the United States was established. Jefferson and his kind were Democratic-Republicans; their opponents were Federalists. Even though the constitution makes no mention of political parties, the system has endured through the centuries. As President, Jefferson master-minded the Louisiana Purchase of 1803, which doubled the size of the United States. In his second term, 1805-1809, he was much less popular than in his first. He was more than happy to retire to his plantation at Monticello in Virginia where he lived out his old age.

MONTICELLO, THE EAST PORTICO.

Monticello means "Little Mountain" in Italian. Jefferson's home was being constantly rebuilt by his slaves, very few of whom he freed when he died.

James Madison
(1751–1836)

★ Fourth President, 1809–1817 ★

A VIRGINIAN, MADISON nonetheless attended the College of New Jersey, later called Princeton University. He served in the Virginia Assembly, in the Continental Congress and played an essential role at the Constitutional Convention of 1787. With John Jay and Alexander Hamilton, Madison wrote the *Federalist* essays which argued in favor of the Constitution. Because of his contributions, he is often called the "Father of the Constitution" in the same way that Washington is called the "Father of his Country." Before being elected President as a Democratic-Republican, Madison served as Jefferson's Secretary of State. As President, he was pressured into declaring war on Great Britain in 1812. This action resulted in disaster for the United States. The British

First Lady, Dorothea Dandridge Payne Todd "Dolley" Madison, 1768–1849.

Jackson victorious at battle of New Orleans.

won most important battles and actually entered Washington D. C. and set the White House on fire. However, the American General Andrew Jackson won an important victory at the Battle of New Orleans *after* the Treaty of Ghent, Belgium ended the war on December 24, 1814. (Communications were very slow in those days.) President Madison's friends used Jackson's victory to convince the American public that the War of 1812 had been successful. Because the Federalists had opposed the war, they were now dismissed as not being supportive of their country. They disappeared as a political party.

James Monroe
(1758–1831)

★ **Fifth President, 1817–1825** ★

THE FIFTH PRESIDENT was the fourth Virginian to hold the highest office in the land. A Democratic-Republican, he had participated in the Constitutional Convention and was Minister to France during Washington's second term. He later served as a United States Senator. With Robert Livingston of New York, he helped negotiate the Louisiana Pur-

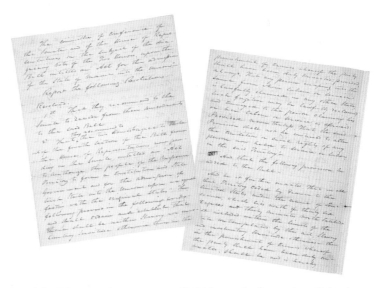

The Missouri Compromise of 1820 was the first serious federal effort to balance the interests of slave states with those where slavery was illegal.

chase for President Jefferson. Early in his first term, Monroe and the country enjoyed what has been called an "Era of Good Feelings," but this goodwill did not last. By appointing as his advisers members from different parts of the coun-

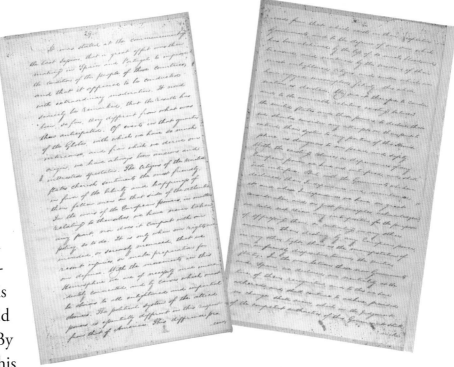

Although its stated purpose was to prevent European powers from further expansion into the American hemisphere, the Monroe Doctrine has also been used by the U. S. government to exert its own influence in Central and South America.

try, he tried to hold the sections of the nation together. The issue of slavery threatened to tear the North and South apart. The Missouri Compromise of 1820 allowed Missouri into the Union as a slave state, balanced by the admission of Maine as a free state. The Compromise made slavery illegal north and west of Missouri forever. Monroe's influence on foreign affairs was great. He asserted that North and South America were no longer open to colonization by European powers. As recently as 1962, President John F. Kennedy referred to the Monroe Doctrine as his authority during a time of national crisis: the Soviet Union had placed missiles in the Communist nation of Cuba, only ninety miles from Florida, and President Kennedy successfully insisted that they be removed.

John Quincy Adams
(1767–1848)

★ **Sixth President, 1825–1829** ★

THE SON OF THE SECOND President of the United States, J. Q. Adams was in many respects the mirror image of his father. Born in Quincy, Massachusetts on the family farm, he followed in his father's footsteps by attending Harvard College and then beginning government service at the age of 26. He learned several languages very early in his life, and mastered even more as he served Presidents Washington and Madison as foreign minister to the Netherlands, Prussia and to the imperial court of Russia. As Secretary of State under President Monroe, he helped draft the Monroe Doctrine. A highly intelligent and polite man, J.Q. Adams did not survive the rough and tumble competition in the election of 1828. The Jacksonian wing of the Democratic-Republican party accused him of corruption, and he was unable to defend himself against those charges. After he lost the election, he returned to Quincy, expecting to live out his life as a country lawyer and gentleman farmer. To the contrary, in 1830 he began 18 years of service in the U. S. Congress. In that role, he fought tirelessly against slavery and suffered a fatal stroke in the House of Representatives.

Andrew Jackson
(1767–1845)

★ **Seventh President, 1829–1837** ★

JACKSON WAS BORN in rural South Carolina and lived in Tennessee when that state was still part of North Carolina. Though he was never educated in school or college, he became financially success-ful as a lawyer, soldier and politician. As a gen-eral in the War of 1812, he won the Battle of New Orleans against the British. He was such a tough and disciplined man that his followers called him "Old Hickory" (a hickory is an espe-cially sturdy tree), a nickname he was proud of for the rest of his life. By 1824 he was suffi-ciently popular that he won a majority of the popular vote in the Presidential election of that year. However, neither he nor his competitors earned a majority of the votes of the Electoral

First Lady, Rachel Donelson Robards Jackson, 1767–1828.

College, and the House of Representatives awarded the presidency to J. Q. Adams, thus fulfilling their constitutional responsibility. Jackson won election easily in 1828 and instantly recommended that the Electoral College be outlawed. He failed in this effort, as has everyone who has since tried. He tried to set up a civil service system so that government jobs would go to qualified applicants, not just to people who had supported a particular elected official.

General Jackson at the Battle of New Orleans.

He tried to write new rules for the Bank of the United States, which he feared no longer responded to the public's needs. His efforts on behalf of the people made him very popular, and he won nearly 56% of the popular vote in the re-election year of 1832.

In 2008 a commemorative $1 coin was issued by the U.S. Mint honoring Andrew Jackson.

Martin Van Buren
(1782–1862)

★ **Eighth President, 1837–1841** ★

T HE FIRST NEW YORKER to become President, Van Buren had worked his way up through the ranks of the Democratic party. He was an important figure in New York State politics and was appointed U. S. Senator in 1821. By 1827 he had become Andrew Jackson's right-hand man in the northern states. When Jackson was elected President in 1828, he appointed Van Buren his Secretary of State. From this vantage point, he was able to serve as Jackson's most trusted adviser. "Old Hickory" referred to him as "a true man," incapable of lying. Elected President in 1836, Van Buren took office in March of 1837, just in time to be blamed for the nation's economic problems that began that year. Across the United States, banks were closed and businesses were bankrupted. People had no jobs and no money. It was a very sad time for the nation, and President Van Buren, as chief executive, was blamed for a lot of the people's troubles. He did try for re-election in 1840, but was defeated.

William Henry Harrison
(1773–1841)

★ **Ninth President, March–April 1841** ★

HARRISON CAUGHT A COLD on his inaugural day, March 4, 1841, and died of pneumonia exactly one month later. When he was elected—the first candidate who was not a Democratic-Republican since the election of John Adams in 1796—the Whig party had rejoiced. Harrison was an outsider, a man who had spent his adult life far from Washington, D. C. For this reason, Whigs believed, the federal government would be more moral than it had been. Whatever Harrison's contributions might or might not have been will never be known. No one could reasonably expect to judge a President's worth based on just thirty days in office, most of them passed in serious illness.

First Lady, Anna Tuthill Symmes Harrison, 1775-1864.

John Tyler
(1790–1862)

★ **Tenth President (1841–1845)** ★

WHEN WILLIAM HENRY HARRISON died after only one month as President, Vice President John Tyler made history by assuming all the powers of an elected President. Since 1841 a number of Presidents have died in office, and the citizens of the United States have grown used to a Vice President automatically becoming President in those cases. However, the federal constitution did not guarantee this until the 25th amendment was passed in 1967. Knowing this, Tyler quickly moved into the White House and did all that he could to become known as "Mr. President." Because he was as much a Whig as Harrison had been, his powerful allies in congress supported him. Soon, however, he lost the support of his own party and the Whigs threw him out. Because of his unpopularity, a resolution was brought against him in the House of Representatives, seeking to have him removed from office. The resolution failed. Tyler added Texas to the United States. In his later life, Tyler tried to reach a compromise between the North and the South when southern states started to secede (withdraw) from the Union in 1861. When his compromise efforts failed, he became a member of the Confederate States Congress.

James Polk
(1795–1849)

★ **Eleventh President, 1845–1849** ★

A MEMBER OF the Democratic party, Polk inherited a huge problem from the Whig administration of Harrison and Tyler: the addition of Texas to the United States. Because Mexico believed Texas to be part of itself, Mexico severed diplomatic relations with the United States. Polk took the United States to war with Mexico. At the end of that conflict, Mexico was forced to give vast areas of its own country, including what are now the states of New Mexico, Arizona and California, to the United States. Polk also vastly expanded the territory of the United States in the Northwest. He and Great Britain peacefully agreed to the present boundary between the U. S. and Canada. Polk was able to persuade the extremists in his government to settle for this boundary, thus avoiding war with England.

First Lady, Sarah Childress Polk, 1803–1891.

Zachary Taylor
(1784–1850)

★ **Twelfth President, 1849–1850** ★

WITH ZACHARY TAYLOR the Whigs did what they had done with William Henry Harrison in 1840. They successfully nominated a military hero, this one from the war against Mexico, and also a Washington outsider. The election of 1848 was interesting because a third party for the first time determined the outcome of the election. Taylor was a slave owner; his Democratic opponent, Lewis Cass, was in favor of letting the territories themselves decide whether to be slave or free. Neither position was acceptable to the "Free Soilers," those who wanted no extension of slavery. This third party nominated former

Major General Zachary Taylor: "rough & ready."

General Taylor on horseback at the Battle of Buena Vista, Mexico, ordering that more ammunition be used against the Mexican army.

President Van Buren, and he pulled enough votes away from Lewis Cass to throw the election to Taylor. Once in office, "Old Rough and Ready" as he was called by his troops, tried his best to free himself from the demands of the Whig leaders in Congress. At the same time, northerners were deeply offended by the presence of a slave market operating in Washington, D. C., a market the President showed no desire to close down. Although a southerner, he was a very strong nationalist. His fellow southerners wanted stronger laws requiring that northerners return to them any slaves who managed to escape from them.

Millard Fillmore
(1800–1874)

★ **Thirteenth President, 1850–1853** ★

Like John Tyler before him, Fillmore came to the presidency by accident, moving into the White House after the death of President Zachary Taylor. These days, he is known only as one of the pre-Civil War Presidents, rather than for anything he did during his brief time in office. In fact, as Vice President, Fillmore controlled the operations of the senate during the debates over the important Compromise of 1850. When he unex-

African American men, women, and children being auctioned off in front of a crowd of men.

pectedly became President in the summer of 1850, he insisted that the Compromise become law. Throughout the life of the United States, Congress had tried to keep the southern states from leaving the Union, and this could be done only by making sure that slavery remained legal. Briefly, the Compromise admitted California as a free state; other lands conquered during the war against Mexico (Utah, Arizona, New Mexico, etc.) were given the right to determine for themselves whether or not to permit slavery; the slave trade was prohibited in the District of Columbia; fugitive slave laws (laws requiring that escaped slaves be returned to their owners) were strengthened. Fillmore and other moderate voices in the government hoped that this Compromise would finally settle the question of slavery. However, only four years later the question appeared once again, and within eleven years of the passing of the Compromise, the South was battling the rest of the country in the American Civil War.

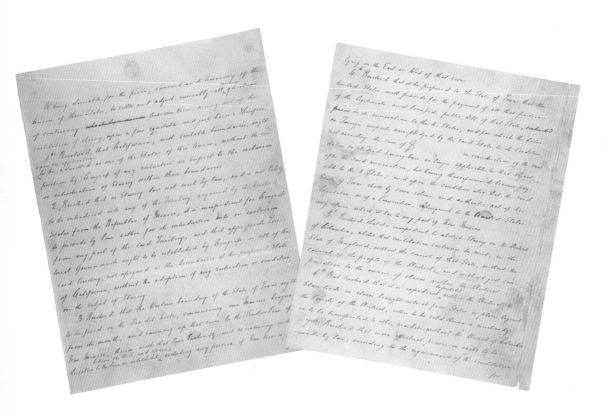

The Compromise of 1850, Millard Fillmore's masterpiece of legislation, tried permanently to balance the interests of slave-holding states against those of free states.

Franklin Pierce
(1804–1869)

★ **Fourteenth President, 1853–1857** ★

T HE COMPROMISE OF **1850** was securely in place when Pierce took office, and the United States enjoyed relative calm. Even though he was a northerner, he took advice from southerners. Because of this, his allies in the north began to doubt his sincerity. For example, he wanted to buy Cuba from Spain, and northerners immediately accused him of wanting to expand American slavery there. Even when he tried to pressure England into leaving its Central American colony of British Honduras (today, the country of Belize), northerners suspected him of trying to expand the territory of the United States. According to his critics, he was simply trying to open up new lands to allow for the growth of slavery. However, it was the Kansas-Nebraska Act of 1854 which

First Lady, Jane Means Pierce, 1806-1863.

THE "MUSTANG" TEAM

The abolitionist Republican presidential ticket and its supporters in the press are mocked for their anti-slavery stance in this political cartoon. A sack marked "Bleeding Kansas Fund" refers to hostilities in Kansas between antislavery and pro-slavery advocates.

destroyed the fragile peace between northern and southern interests. The Act repealed the Missouri Compromise of 1820 and once again opened up the whole question of where slavery might be allowed in the new western territories of the United States. The Act of 1854 allowed citizens of the Kansas and Nebraska territories to be either for or against slavery. In those two areas, especially in "bleeding Kansas" of the late 1850s, many people believe the Civil War of 1861-1865 actually began. By the closing months of his administration, Pierce was able to claim a measure of peace in Kansas, but it was too late to save his political future: the Democrats refused to renominate him in 1856.

James Buchanan
(1791–1868)

★ **Fifteenth President, 1857–1861** ★

A PENNSYLVANIAN, BUCHANAN served five terms in the U. S. House of Representatives and ten years as a Senator. He was also President Polk's Secretary of State and Pierce's Minister to Great Britain. Because he had spent so much of his recent past overseas, he had not become too deeply involved in the bitterness generated by the Compromise of 1850 and by the Kansas-Nebraska Act of 1854. His seeming neutrality on these important issues was very important in gaining him the Democratic nomination for President in 1856. Two days after Buchanan was sworn in as President, the Supreme Court—under the direction of Chief Justice Roger B. Taney—ruled that Congress had no power to deprive slave owners of their "property" in the territories. This infamous Dred Scott decision pleased southerners but enraged northerners. Buchanan was powerless to calm the situation. After the new Republican party won a majority in the mid-term election of 1858, the Federal government, Buchanan included, was able to accomplish nothing. The President's Democratic party split into northern and southern wings, and the candidate of the Republican party, whoever that might be, was assured of winning the Presidential election of 1860.

Dred Scott was a slave owned by a U. S. Army officer in Missouri, a slave state. The officer later moved to Illinois and Wisconsin, both free states, taking Scott with him. The officer moved back to Missouri, where he died. Scott went to court to earn his freedom, based on the fact that he'd lived so many years in free states. His case went all the way up to the U. S. Supreme Court, where seven out of nine of the justices ruled against him, saying that no slave or descendant of a slave could be a citizen, and therefore had no rights. Roger B. Taney, Chief Justice of the Supreme Court, was a former slaveowner from Maryland.

Abraham Lincoln
(1809–1865)

★ **Sixteenth President, 1861–1865** ★

Lincoln is usually ranked second only to Washington among Presidents of the United States. Washington fathered his country; Lincoln insisted that the Union remain united. To accomplish this, he served as Commander-in-Chief of U. S. armed forces during the bloodiest war ever fought by America. The American Civil War denied eleven southern states the right to withdraw from the Union and create a country of their own, the Confederate States of America. On almost exactly the same day that the war ended, Lincoln was assassinated in Washington, D. C. Although never wildly popular during his lifetime, his tragic death helped ensure him a permanent place among the greatest heroes of his country. He was from Illinois, born

First Lady, Mary Todd Lincoln, 1818–1882.

The Emancipation Proclamation of 1863 did not end slavery in the United States; it only declared the freedom of slaves in those states in open rebellion against the authority of the United States.

into terrible poverty. Self-educated, he became a lawyer. He achieved the presidency as the candidate of the new Republican party. His years in the White House were marked by tragedy. Union and Confederate troops died by the hundreds of thousands. Above all, Lincoln kept saying, the

The 1863 Battle of Gettysburg, Pennsylvania, was fought on July 1–3. Union troops won the battle, which was later seen as the time when the Union began to win the Civil War. President Lincoln's commander, Major-General George Meade, refused to push his advantage and capture the retreating Confederate army. The war would continue for nearly two more years.

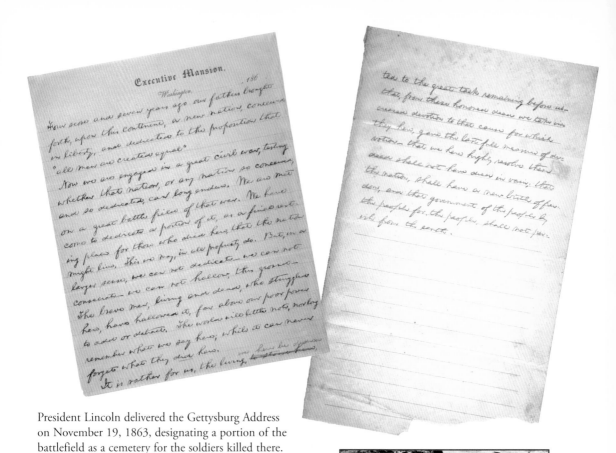

President Lincoln delivered the Gettysburg Address on November 19, 1863, designating a portion of the battlefield as a cemetery for the soldiers killed there.

Union must be preserved. He required his country to pay the highest of prices for the right and privilege of remaining united. As the war continued, Lincoln began to believe that the conflict was about more than just preserving the Union. He listened to northerners who wanted to end slavery in the United States once and for all. (They were called abolitionists because they wanted to "abolish" or end slavery.) On the first day of 1863, he emancipated (freed) the slaves who lived in the Confederate States. Not until after his death, however, did legalized slavery end in the United States.

Above, The presidential box at Ford's Theatre, Washington, D.C. where Lincoln was assassinated on April 14, 1865 by John Wilkes Booth, *right*.

Andrew Johnson
(1808–1875)

★ **Seventeenth President, 1865–1869** ★

A MONG THE MOST UNFORTUNATE of Presidents, Johnson was a decent man caught up in complicated webs of political power and plots. First of all, he served in the shadow of the dead President Lincoln. (In this respect, he was a little like John Adams, the second President, who followed the great Washington.) Second, the radical Republicans had gained control of Congress. Andrew Johnson, a conservative Democrat, got in their way. Johnson followed Lincoln's plan for pardoning everyone in the South who would take an oath of allegiance to the United States. On this model, he began to reconstruct the South, which had nearly been destroyed by the Civil War. This was not good enough for the Republicans. They wanted to punish the South. In the off-

First Lady, Eliza McCardle Johnson, 1810–1876.

year election of 1866, the Republicans won overwhelming majorities in both houses of Congress. They began to ram through any legislation they desired. When Johnson stood in their way, the House impeached him and the Senate failed by just one vote to convict him. The efforts to impeach, convict and remove a President from office are deeply serious matters. Congress would not follow this path again for more than 100 years.

Northern efforts to rebuild or reconstruct the South following the Civil War were often greeted with ridicule. (In fact, those northerners were often crooks and swindlers.) Because they traveled with little luggage, clearly intending not to stay long, southerners dismissed them as "carpetbaggers," people who came to take what they could and leave little of value behind.

Andrew Johnson's impeachment trial before the U.S. Senate, March 30–May 26, 1868.

Ulysses S. Grant
(1822–1885)

★ **Eighteenth President, 1869–1877** ★

Like Generals Harrison in 1840, Taylor in 1848 and Eisenhower in 1952, U. S. Grant was a war hero who was elected President without having had any previous political experience. Grant was President Lincoln's most successful general in the Civil War. He and the President became friends, and Lincoln almost always followed Grant's suggestions. In Lincoln's phrase, only Grant dared "face the arithmetic" of the War. Facing the arithmetic meant that, because the North was so much bigger than the South, the North could afford to lose more soldiers than the South did and still win the War. Unfortunately, Grant was a much more successful general than he was a President. His two terms were marked by scandal, inactivity, and corruption. Though both

First Lady, Julia Dent Grant, 1826–1902.

Lt. Gen. Ulysses S. Grant: General in Chief of the armies of the United States. Lincoln was so grateful to Grant that the President gave him this military title which had previously been held only by Washington.

he and the majority party in Congress were Republican, not much important legislation was introduced or passed during his eight years in office. The radical Republican plan for reconstructing the South continued under his administration, the plan treating the southern states as a conquered nation. This so-called Reconstruction created understandable bitterness in the South. In some counties in the states of the former Confederacy, the U. S. flag did not fly above courthouses again until World War II.

Abraham Lincoln, William Tecumseh Sherman, Philip Henry Sheridan, and Ulysses S. Grant around small table with a map on it. The future President is seated on the far right, next to President Lincoln's other two most successful Generals.

Rutherford B. Hayes
(1822–1893)

★ Nineteenth President 1877–1881 ★

ALTHOUGH A DECENT and honest man, Hayes will be forever remembered as the man who won the most bizarre Presidential election in U. S. history. An

Ohioan, Hayes practiced law in that state and served honorably in the Union army during the Civil War. In the 1860s and '70s he served in the U. S. House of Representatives and as governor of Ohio. In 1876 he ran for President against the Democratic governor of New York, Samuel J. Tilden. As the returns came in, it was obvious that Tilden had won the popular vote, but the 20 electoral votes of Louisiana, South Carolina and Florida were claimed by both Democrats and Republicans. If even one of those electoral votes went to Tilden, he would win; Hayes had to win

First Lady, Lucy Webb Hayes, 1831–1889.

every one of the 20 to claim victory. The election was still not decided by January of 1877, at which time Congress (dominated by the Republicans) created a special Electoral Commission to determine who would win the votes of those three states. There were eight Republicans on the Commission and seven Democrats: the Commission decided by a vote of 8-7 to award all electoral votes to

Chief Justice Morrison R. Waite administering the oath of office to Rutherford B. Hayes on a flag-draped inaugural stand on the east portico of the U.S. Capitol, March 4, 1877.

Hayes. He won by a total of 185 electoral votes to 184 for Tilden.

James A. Garfield
(1831–1881)

★ **Twentieth President, 1881** ★

GARFIELD WAS A MUCH more radical Republican than Lincoln was. However, Lincoln and he were friends. Lincoln asked him to give up his officer's rank in the army to become a Representative, telling Garfield that it was much easier for him to find major generals than it was to find friendly members of Congress. As a member of the U. S. House of Representatives, Garfield advocated using any force necessary to return the southern states to the Union. Garfield won the Presidential election of 1880 by fewer than 10,000 popular votes. He became the second American President to be assassinated, less than two decades after the murder of President Lincoln. He might have been an effective President. He had, for example, invited the Presi-

First Lady, Lucretia Rudolph Garfield, 1832–1918.

dents of all the other American republics to meet in Washington, D. C. in 1882, but of course his death prevented that conference from taking place.

Gen. James Abraham Garfield.

The attack on the President's life at the Baltimore and Ohio Railroad depot in Washington. The arrest of the assassin in the background.

Chester Alan Arthur
(1829–1886)

★ Twenty-first President, 1881–1885 ★

BORN IN VERMONT, ARTHUR BECAME a life-long New Yorker. A graduate of Union College in Albany, he practiced law in New York City and associated himself with the Republican political "machine" of the famous (or infamous) Roscoe Conkling. Oddly enough, though personally honest, Arthur believed in the spoils system as administered by Conkling. In effect, this system imitated the practice of imperial Rome: when the Roman army won a victory, they took the prizes, the "spoils" of war. In Nineteenth-century terms, this meant that the party in office (the winners) were able to give jobs to their loyal followers. Even during President Garfield's brief term of office, when he was serving as Vice President, Arthur stood with Con-

First Lady, Ellen Herndon Arthur, 1837–1880.

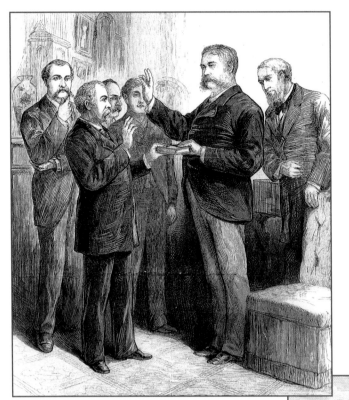

kling against his own President. Interestingly enough, when he became President, Arthur changed his mind and began favoring civil service reform. The Pendleton Act of 1883 set up a system of awarding government jobs according to merit, not according to the spoils system. President Arthur was not renominated by his party for a second term in 1884.

Justice John R. Brady, Justice of the New York State Supreme Court, administering the oath of office to Vice President Arthur in a private ceremony in Arthur's residence at 123 Lexington Avenue, New York.

President Arthur and his party on the Brooklyn Bridge, 1883.

Grover Cleveland
(1837–1908)

★ *Twenty-second President, 1885–1889* ★
and
Twenty-fourth President, 1893–1897

CLEVELAND WAS THE FIRST Democrat elected after the Civil War and the only President ever to serve non-consecutive terms. Although he was obviously only one person, he is always considered to have served two presidencies. He was born and died in New Jersey, but came to manhood and political maturity in New York. He was elected mayor of Buffalo and then Governor of New York. As President he was extremely conservative and frequently rejected efforts on the part of Congress to aid various groups of the country. He did not want federal aid to go to Texas farmers whose farms suffered

First Lady, Frances Cornelia Folsom Cleveland, 1864–1947.

from drought. Such aid, he said, would weaken the national character of Americans. He denied veterans' benefits to many former Civil War soldiers, thus angering a lot of people. When railroad workers went on strike, he sent

A dynamite bomb exploding among the police at the Haymarket Square Riot in Chicago during the McCormick Strike, 1886.

in federal troops to force them back to work. His second term, 1893–1897, was dominated by a Depression which began in its first year. In foreign affairs, he was able to negotiate a boundary dispute between Venezuela and the British colony of Guyana in South America. Although he was willing to run for a third term in 1896, the Democrats turned away from him and nominated William Jennings Bryan instead.

Statue of Liberty partly clouded by smoke from military and naval salute marking President Grover Cleveland's arrival at Liberty Island (1886); steamboats in foreground: "Magnolia" and "Myndert Starin."

Benjamin Harrison
(1833–1901)

★ Twenty-third President, 1889–1893 ★

O NLY 5'6" TALL, Benjamin Harrison was sometimes called "Little Ben," a nickname he hated. A Midwesterner from Ohio and Indiana, he served in the Civil War as an officer and then went to Washington D. C. as a Republican senator from Indiana. His endless work for the Republican party, combined with his reputation as a man of high moral standing, won him his party's nomination for President in 1888. Although he lost the popular vote to Grover Cleveland, he won the presidency by winning enough electoral votes. He had made no bargains to win the presidency, but his supporters had pledged a lot of jobs to a lot of people if they would support Harrison's effort. Because of this, he entered his presidency under a cloud of suspicion. He was

First Lady, Caroline Lavinia Scott Harrison, 1832–1892.

very proud of his achievements in foreign affairs. For example, the first Pan American Congress met in Washington in 1889. This great institution still exists, nowadays known as the Pan-American Union. He was renominated by his party in 1892 but was defeated by Cleveland.

General Benjamin Harrison in uniform, on horseback, leading a brigade of soldiers in the Civil War Battle of Resaca, May 13th to 16th 1864.

Caricature of President Benjamin Harrison, as a very short person, with large head, seated at a desk, wearing the big hat of his grandfather William Henry Harrison, also a president. On a bust perches Secretary of State James G. Blaine, shown as a raven, presumably croaking "Nevermore." President Harrison's own Secretary of State often opposed his policies, making life in the White House very difficult for Harrison.

William McKinley
(1843–1901)

★ **Twenty-fifth President, 1897–1901** ★

WHEN MCKINLEY WAS elected President in 1896, he was accused by his enemies of being the puppet of a wealthy Cleveland businessman named Marc Hanna. To be sure, Hanna supported McKinley, but it is also true that, by 1896, McKinley had proven himself independent. He had served fourteen years in the U. S. House of Representatives where he had earned the respect of his colleagues. As Governor of Ohio, he was popular and well-liked. In fact McKinley was so likeable that he didn't even bother to campaign for the presidency. Rather, he sat on his front porch in Canton, Ohio, visiting with voters who passed by to say hello. He won the presidency with the largest percentage of the popular vote since Grant's re-election in 1872. His four-

First Lady, Ida Saxton McKinley, 1847–1907.

and-a-half years as President were dominated by foreign affairs. He fought a brief war against Spain in 1898 at the end of which he took control of the Spanish colonies of Puerto Rico, the Philippines, Guam, and Cuba. Guam and Puerto Rico are owned by the United States to this day. Mark Twain and other American writers and thinkers were disgusted by the President's empire-building, but McKinley's actions were approved by large majorities of the American people. He was assassinated early in his second term.

In this political cartoon, the father of Philippine independence, Emilio Aguinaldo (1869–1964), is only an "insurgent" (rebel) mosquito being swatted by President McKinley.

Assassination of President McKinley—Leon Czolgosz, a political radical, shoots President McKinley with a concealed revolver, at the Pan-American Exposition reception, Sept. 6th, 1901.

Theodore Roosevelt
(1858–1919)

★ **Twenty-sixth President, 1901–1909** ★

AT FIRST PEOPLE WERE fearful that a man so young—Teddy Roosevelt was not quite 43 when he became President—could govern effectively, but he soon showed the American public that he was not just an accidental President. Born into a wealthy New York City family, he spent many years of his youth as a rancher in South Dakota. He did not enjoy good physical health and tried very hard to improve himself physically. He fought in Cuba during the Spanish-American War of 1898, leading a regiment of soldiers known as the Rough Riders. Not subject to modesty, he made sure that his adventures made it into the newspapers back home. He was later Governor of New York and then ran as Vice President with McKinley during that Presi-

First Lady, Edith Kermit Carow Roosevelt, 1861–1948.

Theodore Roosevelt in Rough Rider uniform.

dent's re-election bid of 1900. He fathered the Panama Canal; he made sure that the older nations of the world saw America as a competitor and friend worthy of respect. He was a conservationist who founded the system of National Parks. At the same time, he probably killed more wild animals than any other famous person ever has. An exciting speaker, he loved being President. He respected the constitution, though also admitted, "I did greatly broaden the use of executive power." He returned to presidential politics as a third-party candidate in 1912, three years after leaving office as a Republican President.

President Theodore Roosevelt on steam-powered digging machine during construction of the Panama Canal, 1908.

William Howard Taft
(1857–1930)

★ *Twenty-seventh President, 1909–1913* ★

TAFT'S GREATEST PERSONAL JOY came not from having been President but from his nine years as Chief Justice of the United States Supreme Court, a position he held from 1921 until his death in 1930. In fact, after he became Chief Justice, he said, "I don't remember that I was ever President." He was a man who loved the law. He graduated from Yale and became a Federal circuit judge before he was 35. He served both Presidents McKinley and Roosevelt and was hand-picked by the latter to run on the Republican ticket for President in 1908. His respect for the law was probably the reason for his break with Roosevelt. The older President was capable of bending the rules more than a little in order to achieve his goals. In Taft's words, Roosevelt should have

First Lady, Helen Louise Herron Taft, 1861–1943.

"admitted the legal way of reaching the same ends" more often. During Taft's administration the Congress sent off to the states two constitutional amendments, one establishing a Federal income tax and the other ordering that U. S. Senators be elected by the citizens, not appointed by state legislatures.

During Taft's campaign for the presidency in 1908, a political cartoon appeared in Judge magazine. The cartoon character looks up at Taft and says, "You're big enough to have your own policies—and they are good enough for the American people." In this way the Judge shows how Taft's policies are at least as good as those of Teddy Roosevelt.

The U.S. Supreme Court Justices in 1925—*left to right, top to bottom:* Edward Terry Sanford, George Sutherland, Pierce Butler, Harlan Fiske Stone, James Clark McReynolds, Oliver Wendell Holmes, Chief Justice William Howard Taft, Willis Van Devanter, Louis Dembitz Brandeis.

Woodrow Wilson
(1856–1924)

★ **Twenty-eighth President, 1913–1921** ★

MANY PEOPLE BELIEVE that Wilson was never suited to be President. Raised in an academic household—his father was a minister and professor—he was himself a highly educated, sensitive person to whom the rough-and-tumble world of politics seemed unwelcoming. However, his rise to the presidency was fast, almost sudden. He was elected Governor of New Jersey in 1910. That was his very first election, and he was elected President just two years later. In 1912 Theodore Roosevelt had come out of retirement to challenge the Republican President Taft. In the three-way election, Wilson earned more votes than either of his two competitors and was thus elected. His presidency was dominated by World War I, which ran its course in Europe

First Lady, Ellen Louise Axson Wilson, 1860–1914.

between 1914 and 1918. Finally, Wilson took the U. S. to war in 1917. After the War, he tried desperately to get the United States to enter the League of Nations, but the Senate would not agree with him. He worked so hard to gain the country's approval of the League that his health collapsed and he served out the rest of his second term as a very sick man. Not until 1945 would the United States help form the United Nations, the organization of nations which continues its work in the world today.

World War I Poster showing a young woman clutching an American flag as she calls out, with Red Cross symbol and U.S. Capitol in background.

President Woodrow Wilson asking Congress to declare war on Germany, April 2, 1917.

Warren G. Harding

(1865–1923)

★ Twenty-ninth President, 1921–1923 ★

ONE OF HARDING'S Democratic opponents dismissed the Republican President's speeches as a collection of arrogant "phrases moving across the landscape in search of an idea." Indeed, Harding was one of those politicians who mastered the technique of using big words and high-sounding phrases to say very little. Like all politicians, Harding realized that what he said could come back to haunt him, so he did what many politicians still do: he avoided being specific. Although the President was personally honorable, many of the members of his administration were corrupted by power. They

First Lady, Florence Mabel Kling deWolfe Harding, 1860–1924.

Warren G. Harding (right) with General John Joseph "Blackjack" Pershing, commander of the American Expeditionary Force during World War I.

used their official positions to enrich themselves and their friends. His Secretary of Commerce, the future President Hoover, urged the President to expose official wrongdoing, but the President was afraid to do so. He died in August of 1923. Soon after that the scandals of his administration were made public. He was not responsible for everything that went wrong, but most historians agree that his administration was the most corrupt since that of Ulysses S. Grant.

Funeral cortege for President Harding with the north portico entrance to the White House in the background.

Calvin Coolidge
(1872–1933)

★ **Thirtieth President, 1923–1929** ★

PRESIDENT COOLIDGE WAS a tower of respectability in both his public and his private life. As much as people might disagree with his conservative policies, no one could say that he was a liar or a cheat. He restored the confidence of the public in the presidency after the corruption of President Harding's administration. Coolidge was famous for his low-key personality: one of his most famous nicknames is "Silent Cal." A young woman seated next to him at dinner bet that she could get him to say more than three words. The President said only, "You lose." This alone sets him apart from politicians who prefer talking to listening. As a conservative Republican, he believed that the businesses and industries of America would best serve the people of the coun-

First Lady, Grace Goodhue
Coolidge, 1879–1957.

try if they were free of government regulation and interference. He was not seen as a friend of farmers or workers. Although he called for limited aid to farmers in 1923, he later said no to farm relief bills and refused to provide federal funds for producing inexpensive electric power on the Tennessee

Four adults and six children, from Passaic, N.J., picket the White House following President Coolidge's refusal to listen to their complaints about wage cuts in the textile industry.

River. His popularity continued throughout his time in office. He would almost certainly have been re-elected to a second full term in 1928, but chose not to run.

Above: Charles A. Lindbergh, with his plane, "Spirit of St. Louis," in which he had made the first non-stop, solo, Transatlantic fight.

Left: Col. Lindbergh and his mother with the President and Mrs. Coolidge.

Herbert Hoover
(1874–1964)

★ **Thirty-first President, 1929–1933** ★

HOOVER WAS ONE of the most capable administrators ever to occupy the White House. Trained as an engineer, he carried into his public life the techniques and skills he had developed in his profession: analysis of problems and the best way to solve them. Unfortunately for him, and tragically for the country, his administration got underway just six months before the Great Depression began in October of 1929. The Depression was unfairly blamed on him, and he was destroyed politically. He lost the 1932 election by just about exactly the same overwhelming majority with which he had won the election of 1928. He was himself a thoroughly decent man, one of the few honest men to work in the upper levels of the Harding administration. With

First Lady, Lou Henry Hoover, 1874–1944.

President Coolidge, he helped restore the public's confidence in the presidency after the Harding administration. After he was forcibly retired from politics, he was appointed by both Presidents Truman (a Democrat) and Eisenhower (a Republican) to direct important Presidential commissions. Throughout the decades, no matter the political party of the President in power, he was so well trusted that he worked for every U. S. President from Wilson to Eisenhower, with the exception of Franklin Delano Roosevelt.

During the Depression, New York City residents desperate for cash sell their possessions at the Houston St. Junk markets, March 10, 1933.

An impoverished family of nine on a New Mexico highway. Depression refugees from Iowa. Nine children including a sick four-month-old baby. No money at all, 1936 .

During the Depression many farms were foreclosed on and farmers who had no place to live moved to towns and cities. Population centers were surrounded by villages of shacks, called "Hoovervilles" as an insult to the President. Willamette River, Portland, Oregon, 1936.

Franklin Delano Roosevelt
(1882–1945)

★ **Thirty-second President, 1933–1945** ★

DURING **FDR'S LONG ADMINISTRATION**—twelve years and three months—America survived twin threats: the economic depression which began in 1929 and the military aggression of Germany, Italy and Japan in Europe, Africa and Asia which resulted in World War II. For eight years, FDR tried through various non-military means to end the Depression before the war began in 1941. Most historians agree that only U. S. involvement in World War II, with all the industrial development the war effort required, brought an end to the Depression. Before the war began, Roosevelt created the Civilian Conservation Corps and the Works Progress Administration in order to provide government-sponsored employment for Americans. Under him,

First Lady, Anna Eleanor Roosevelt, 1884–1962.

Roosevelt created the WPA (Works Progress Administration) and the CCC (Civilian Conservation Corps) to attempt to stimulate the economy during the Great Depression. He also presided over the founding of the Social Security system.

Social Security payments became a fact of life for retired Americans. When the Supreme Court ruled some of his measures unconstitutional, he responded by trying to "pack" the court with judges friendly to his efforts. This was one of the low points of his administration. Another was his decision to allow Japanese-Americans to be removed from their homes and businesses on the West

On December 7, 1941 the Japanese Imperial Navy launched a sneak attack against the U.S. fleet based at Pearl Harbor, Hawaii. This act of aggression drew the United States into World War II, and was referred to by FDR in his famous speech as "a date which will live in infamy."

Coast and detained in camps during World War II. Whatever his weaknesses as a politician, he was one of the essential American Presidents. Like Washington at the founding of the country and Lincoln during the Civil War, FDR remained true to his vision of America. Intelligent and politically active, his wife Eleanor was also a force to be reckoned with. Among other things, she insisted that her husband begin thinking of ways to achieve racial equality in the United States.

President Roosevelt signing the declaration of war against Germany, Dec. 11, 1941.

Prime Minister Winston Churchill, President Franklin D. Roosevelt, and Marshal Joseph Stalin at the palace in Yalta in February of 1945, where the "Big Three" met to plan the allied efforts.

Roosevelt died in office on April 12, 1945, too soon to see the ultimate allied victory. Here, his funeral procession moves down Pennsylvania Ave. with horse-drawn casket.

Harry S. Truman
(1884–1972)

★ **Thirty-third President, 1945–1953** ★

TRUMAN WAS **FDR's** third Vice President and had served in that job for only a few weeks when he suddenly became President upon Roosevelt's death. Truman imagined himself to be like John Adams following the great Washington or Andrew Johnson coming to the presidency after Lincoln. He was always true to himself and to his principles. One might agree or disagree with him, but one always knew his position on any given topic. He was plain-speaking. Born in Missouri, of a humble family, Truman served as a soldier in Europe during World War I and then failed at farming and at store-keeping. He got into politics, served in the U. S. Senate and then was tapped by the Democrats to run with FDR in 1944. He did not have time to get to know

First Lady, Bess Wallace Truman, 1885–1982.

the President. Only after Roosevelt's death did he learn about the existence of the atomic bomb; he approved its use against the Japanese cities of Hiroshima and Nagasaki in August of 1945, at the very end of World War II. He never apologized for taking this horrific action, and historians still disagree about whether dropping the bombs brought a quicker end to the war, thus saving lives. Truman was re-elected in 1948 to everyone's surprise but his own, besting the popular New York Governor Thomas Dewey by 303 electoral votes to 189.

Truman authorized the atomic bombing of Hiroshima and Nagasaki, Japan in order to end World War II without an invasion of the Japanese mainland, which could have resulted in over a million American casualties according to War Department projections.

Truman's tenure as president saw U.S. involvement in the Korean War (1950–53). General Douglas MacArthur—shown here consulting with his staff at the front lines above Suwon, Korea—was the commander of all United Nations forces in the conflict.

Dwight D. Eisenhower
(1890–1969)

★ **Thirty-fourth President, 1953–1961** ★

As COMMANDER-IN-CHIEF of Allied forces in Europe during the final phase of World War II, Eisenhower took responsibility for the liberation of Europe that began on June 6, 1944. The army, air force and naval units that participated in this invasion made up the greatest single military effort the world had ever seen. The movement from England across the Channel was a success, and the troops of Hitler and his allies were driven back across the map of Europe. Had Eisenhower's plans failed, World War II might have lasted until 1950 or 1951, rather than ending in 1945. This would have meant horrible suffering and death for hundreds of thousands more people, soldiers and civilians alike. In civilian life after the war, Eisenhower occupied himself in

First Lady, Mamie Geneva Doud Eisenhower, 1896–1979.

various jobs, including brief service as the President of Columbia University. A man whose personal life was always free of scandal, his heroism as a famous general made him the natural choice of the Republican party for the election of 1952. In office, he bravely confronted the two outstanding crises of his day. In foreign affairs, this meant preventing the spread of Soviet communism during what history calls "the Cold War." The second crisis was on the domestic front and involved African-Americans finally beginning to achieve the civil rights they had been promised in the constitutional amendments adopted following the Civil War.

Eisenhower's presidency saw the blossoming of an arms race that characterized much of the Cold War era. ICBMs were deployed extensively by both the Soviets and the U.S. in a strategy that became known as "Mutually Assured Destruction."

U2 spy planes were used extensively to track the development of Soviet missile capabilities using aerial photography. One of the tensest moments of the cold war occurred when one of the American U2s was brought down by a missile and its pilot, Francis Gary Powers, was captured by the Soviets. Here Soviet leader Nikita Kruschev views a display of items collected from the wreckage.

John F. Kennedy
(1917–1963)

★ **Thirty-fifth President, 1961–1963** ★

KNOWN TO EVERYONE by his monogram, JFK, Kennedy was born into a wealthy and famous Massachusetts family. His father, Joseph Kennedy, had served as the U. S. ambassador to Great Britain before and during part of World War II. JFK and his numerous brothers and sisters thus had the experience of living in a country other than their own. During World War II, JFK served in the Pacific as a naval officer and was seriously wounded. Returning to his country, he made a long, slow recovery, served in the U. S. House of Representatives and was a Senator from Massachusetts when he was elected President by a tiny majority in 1960. As President, he continued battling on the two fronts President Eisenhower had established. The Cold War heated

First Lady, Jacqueline Lee Bouvier Kennedy, 1929–1994.

above: The March on Washington, Aug. 28, 1963.

left: Kennedy meets in the Oval Office with the Leaders of the March On Washington. L-R: Secretary of Labor Willard Wirtz, Mathew Ahmann, Rev. Dr. Martin Luther King, Jr., John Lewis, Rabbi Joachim Prinz, Rev. Eugene Carson Blake, A. Philip Randolph, President Kennedy, Vice President Johnson, Walter Reuther, Whitney Young, Floyd McKissick.

above: Kennedy inspects the interior of the "Friendship 7" Mercury capsule with Astronaut Col. John Glenn, Jr. Cape Canaveral, Florida.

left: The launch of "Freedom 7" carrying Alan Shepard on the first American manned space flight, May 5, 1961.

up and nearly became a shooting war when JFK insisted that the Soviet Union remove its missiles from the communist nation of Cuba in October of 1962. On the home front, President Kennedy continued working for civil rights for African-Americans, though the most significant legislation in this respect was passed after his death. On November 22, 1963, he was assassinated in Dallas, Texas, just about 1,000 days into his administration.

Adlai Stevenson presented aerial photos of Cuban missiles to the United Nations Security Council in November 1962. U2 spy plane photos like the one above effectively countered Soviet denials.

left: President and Mrs. Kennedy begin the fateful motorcade ride in which he is assassinated in Dallas.

below left: Mrs. Kennedy and her children leave the Capitol building, where the President lies in state.

below: Procession to St. Matthew's Cathedral.

Lyndon B. Johnson
(1908–1973)

★ **Thirty-sixth President, 1963–1969** ★

Aᴌᴛʜᴏᴜɢʜ ʜᴇ ʙᴇᴄᴀᴍᴇ President only because John Kennedy had been killed in office, Johnson later achieved fame as a President in his own right. Of rural Texas beginnings, he was ultimately elected President in 1964 by the biggest majority of popular votes in U. S. history. He learned the world of politics from the ground up, serving as a Democrat in the House of Representatives during the presidency of Franklin Roosevelt. As a senator he became a highly effective politician. When the Republicans were in power, he worked well with them. When his own party controlled the Senate, he was able to bring Republicans into the decision-making process as much as possible.   As President he rammed through huge packages of legislation aimed at elim-

First Lady, Claudia Alta "Lady Bird" Taylor Johnson, 1912–2007.

inating poverty and racism in America. He was so powerful and popular that scarcely anyone dared oppose him. As a political liberal, he believed that government could do a good deal more for its citizens. Under his direction, for example, Congress created Medicare in 1965. This program currently provides health care to millions of elderly Americans. History worked against LBJ, though. The dissatisfaction of

Johnson takes the oath of office on Air Force One shortly after President Kennedy is assassinated.

Black Americans erupted in riots in the Black neighborhoods of American cities in the mid-1960s. At the same time, those opposed to America's involvement in Vietnam became so numerous that LBJ could no longer ignore them. On March 31, 1968, he announced that he would not seek re-election that fall.

President Lyndon B. Johnson signs the 1968 Civil Rights Bill while seated at a table surrounded by members of Congress.

President Johnson and Rev. Dr. Martin Luther King, Jr. confer in the Cabinet Room of the White House.

Vietnam War protesters outside White House gates, including Coretta Scott King and Dr. Benjamin Spock.

Richard M. Nixon
(1913–1994)

★ **Thirty-seventh President, 1969–1974** ★

NIXON WAS PRESIDENT EISENHOWER'S Vice President but was narrowly defeated by John F. Kennedy in the presidential election of 1960. Except for an unsuccessful attempt to become Governor of California in 1964, he almost disappeared from public life. His comeback in 1968 was greeted as a political miracle. President Nixon unsuccessfully sought to heal the divisions in the country created by opposition to the Vietnam war: the United States remained in place in Vietnam, and opposition to the war increased at home. Nonetheless, Nixon defeated the Democratic candidate, George McGovern, by an overwhelming majority in 1972, and celebrated his popularity. Unfortunately, it was later revealed that he had participated in criminal

First Lady, Thelma Catherine Ryan "Pat" Nixon, 1912–1993.

behavior in the Watergate scandal. He was threatened with impeachment by the House of Representatives in 1974 and would have been convicted by the House and removed from office by the Senate had he not resigned in August, 1974. Few people doubt Nixon's sincerity. Sadly, though, he believed that the ends justified the means: his remaining in office, he believed, had to be achieved by any means, including illegal ones. In his favor, history will always remember that he opened the door to diplomatic and trade relations with China in 1972. He conducted successful high level meetings with Leonid Brezhnev of the Soviet Union, producing treaties which limited the number of nuclear weapons each country could maintain. Despite all his successes in foreign policy, he will always be remembered as the man who said, "I am not a crook," only to be shown to be a liar in that respect.

Nixon at the Great Wall during his visit to China in 1972.

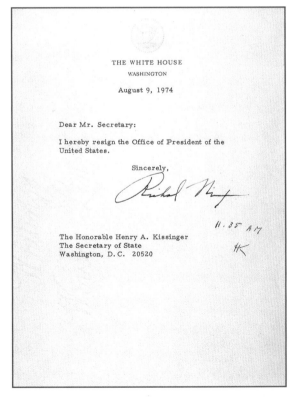

Richard Nixon was the only U.S. President ever to resign from office.

Gerald R. Ford

(1913–2006)

★ **Thirty-eighth President, 1974–1977** ★

BOTH PRESIDENTS FORD AND REAGAN died at 93, although Ford was six weeks older than Reagan was at the time of his death. Thus, Ford had achieved the greatest age of any ex-President. At the time of his funeral, distinguished people and ordinary citizens alike remembered him fondly. He had come into the presidency quite by accident. As a twenty-five year member of the House of Representatives, he had been appointed Vice President by President Nixon when his first Vice President, Spiro Agnew, had resigned in disgrace in 1973. Later, when Nixon resigned the presidency, Ford had become President, having been elected neither President nor Vice President. A decent man, Ford stepped into the presidency as leader of a country

First Lady, Elizabeth Ann Bloomer Warren "Betty" Ford, 1918–.

★ 97

exhausted by the scandals and disgraces of the Nixon administration. Americans were relieved not to read in the newspaper each morning about new crimes and cover-ups. However, the economic condition of the country was not good. People could not afford to live their daily lives happily. Because of this, Presi-

President Ford announces his decision to pardon former President Richard Nixon.

dent Ford was not re-elected in his own right in the election of 1976. However, in the first sentence of his inaugural address on January 20, 1977, President Jimmy Carter offered him this high compliment: "For myself and for our Nation, I want to thank my predecessor for all he has done to heal our land."

The Vietnam War finally ended with the Fall of Saigon during Ford's term in office. American helicopters performed a massive airlift, labeled "Operation Frequent Wind," to evacuate Americans and key Vietnamese personnel. So many helicopters were needed that excess equipment was pushed into the sea to make room for the additional evacuees arriving.

Jimmy Carter
(1924–)

★ **Thirty-ninth President, 1977–1981** ★

JIMMY CARTER ALMOST NEVER used his full name, James Earl Carter, Jr., preferring the nickname "Jimmy." This down-home touch was evident also on his inauguration day, January 20, 1977, when he and his wife left their limousine and walked down Pennsylvania Avenue during the inaugural parade. A Georgian, Carter came to the presidency after a hard-fought, two-year campaign. Not only was he a relative unknown, his task was very difficult in that he had to win against a seated President, Gerald Ford. This he managed to do, winning 297 electoral votes to Ford's 241. Economic woes continued at home, and Americans were still not comfortable with their incomes. In foreign affairs, the high point of Carter's administration was probably the Camp

First Lady, Eleanor Rosalynn Smith Carter, 1927–.

★ 99

David agreement of 1978. At that time, the leaders of Egypt and Israel decided to practice peace rather than war between their two nations. Sadly for Carter, more than 14 months of his administration were dominated by Iran's seizure of U. S. Embassy personnel in Teheran. These American hostages

Anwar Sadat of Egypt and Menachem Begin of Israel shake hands before their first meeting at the Camp David Summit while Jimmy Carter and Rosalynn Carter look on.

were not freed until the day Carter left office. In his post-Presidential life, Carter became a well-known humanitarian, traveling the world in an ongoing effort to ensure free and fair elections in other countries. In 2002 he was awarded the Nobel Peace Prize. At home, he has been a member of the Habitat for Humanity program, helping build houses for poor families.

Nobel Peace Prize Ceremony, Oslo City Hall, Dec. 10, 2002.

Ronald Reagan
(1911–2004)

★ **Fortieth President, 1981–1989** ★

I**N 1980** R**ONALD** R**EAGAN** defeated President Carter by a huge majority, 489 electoral votes to 49 for Carter. President Reagan came into office on a high tide of good feelings. He was popular and likeable; his optimism caught on with the citizens of his country and he was able to get most of his legislation passed by Congress. In 1984 he was re-elected by an even bigger majority, 525 electoral votes to 13 for former Vice President Walter Mondale. The "Reagan Revolution" attempted to restore America's confidence in herself. To this end, he wanted to reverse the trend toward what has been called "big government," the belief and practice of asking governments to provide more and more services to citizens. A political conservative, President Reagan sought to decrease Ameri-

First Lady, Nancy Davis Reagan, 1921–.

above: Reagan walking to his waiting limo on March 30, 1981, the day he was shot and wounded by John Hinckley, Jr.

right: Immediately after the shots were fired.

left: "Challenger" launch.

above: The crew of "Challenger"— Back row, left to right: Ellison Onizuka, Christa McAuliffe, Gregory Jarvis, and Judith Resnik.
Front row, left to right: Michael J. Smith, Dick Scobee, and Ronald McNair.

left: The explosion of the Space Shuttle "Challenger," 73 seconds after launch, January 28, 1986.

Ronald Reagan met with Soviet Prime Minister Gorbachev many times in the interest of nuclear arms reductions. *Left*: at their first summit in Geneva, November 1985. They would meet again in, Reykjavik, Iceland; Washington D.C.; and Moscow. *Above*: signing the INF (Intermediate-Range Nuclear Forces) Treaty, Dec. 8, 1987.

cans' reliance on government. He emphasized the need for a healthy capitalist economy. In foreign affairs Reagan was extremely active, meeting with world leaders regularly and trying in every way he could to re-establish America's role as a world leader. In a famous challenge to the leader of the Soviet Union, he demanded that the wall separating East from West Germany be torn down. He declared war against international terrorism, bombing Libya after it was proved that that country had helped attack American soldiers in Berlin. In all, his eight years in office were highly successful. His two terms saw America enjoy an extended period of peacetime prosperity. Though in his late seventies at the end of his term, he has earned a place in history as one of America's most vigorous Presidents.

Flanked here by former Republican Sen. John Tower and former Democratic Sen. Edmund Muskie, Reagan receives the Tower Report in February, 1987, a document highly critical of his policy of selling arms to Iran. Money from those sales was then secretly funneled to the rebel forces in Nicaragua which were seeking to overthrow their elected Marxist government.

George H. W. Bush
(1924–)

★ **Forty-first President, 1989–1993** ★

PRESIDENT GEORGE HERBERT WALKER BUSH is only the second U. S. President to father another President, in this case, George W. Bush. (John Adams, the second President, was father of John Quincy Adams, the sixth.) Of a famous Connecticut political family, Bush left New England for Texas early in his maturity. He worked in the oil industry for a time, then ran successfully for the U. S. House of Representatives before being asked by Ronald Reagan to run as his Vice Presidential candidate in 1980. After Reagan's presidency, Bush easily won the contest against the Democratic candidate, Governor Michael Dukakis of Massachusetts, in 1988. He then rode a roller coaster of popularity during his four years in office. Because of his

First Lady, Barbara Pierce Bush, 1925–.

effective response to Iraq President Saddam Hussein's aggression against Kuwait in 1990-91, Bush earned one of the highest approval ratings ever achieved by an American President. He carefully built an alliance of countries who joined with the U. S. to drive the Iraqi army out of

President and Mrs. Bush walk with U. S. troops toward mess hall in Saudi Arabia, Thanksgiving Day, November 22, 1990.

Kuwait. When this war had been successfully completed in the spring of 1991, President Bush seemed to most analysts to be certainly re-elected in 1992. In fact, so great was his popularity that none of the major Democratic candidates even bothered to prepare campaigns to run against him. Unfortunately for Bush,

domestic realities, primarily the weakening economy, worked against him, and Bill Clinton succeeded in taking the presidency from him in 1992.

President Bush with the Emir of Kuwait, Jabir Al-Ahmad Al Jabir Al-Sabah in the Oval Office of the White House to discuss the situation in the Gulf.

Bill Clinton
(1946–)

★ Forty-second President, 1993–2001 ★

BILL CLINTON CAME TO THE PRESIDENCY from the governorship of Arkansas. He had been educated at Georgetown University and won a Rhodes Scholarship to Oxford University before returning to Arkansas. Through hard work and awesome powers of organization, he won the Democratic nomination in 1992, in some measure because more famous Democrats were unwilling to run the risk of competing with the popular President George H. W. Bush. Bush's popularity declined in the final year of his administration, and Clinton won the presidency by 370 to 168 electoral votes. Running against Senator Robert Dole in 1996, Clinton was re-elected by an even greater majority, 379 to 159. Like President Reagan before him, Bill Clinton enjoyed great pop-

First Lady, Hillary Rodham Clinton, 1947–.

above: Clinton at the signing of the Dayton–Paris Agreement ending the war in Bosnia and Herzegovina.

right: President Clinton visiting with U.S. peacekeeping troops in Bosnia.

ularity. Unlike Reagan, however, Clinton's private life gave his enemies many reasons to hate him. Congress impeached him in 1998 because he had lied about his relationship with a young woman. The Senate did not convict him, however, and he ended his two terms in office with an approval rating higher than Reagan's. Few people would have predicted this outcome, but economic prosperity made most Americans happy, and citizens were willing to ignore the unpleasant realities of his private life. Under President Clinton the federal government generated budget surpluses, and America enjoyed the lowest unemployment rate in modern times.

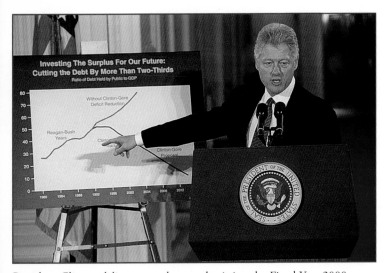

President Clinton delivers remarks on submitting the Fiscal Year 2000 Budget at an event in the East Room of the White House. He points to a chart titled: "Investing the Surplus for our Future: Cutting the Debt by More Than Two-Thirds."

George W. Bush
(1946–)

★ **Forty-third President (2001–2009)** ★

THE SON OF PRESIDENT GEORGE H. W. BUSH, President George W. Bush was born in Connecticut and educated at Yale and Harvard. Moving to Texas where his father and mother had taken up residence, President Bush tried his hand at business before becoming Governor of Texas in 1994. In 2000 he was the Republican nominee for President and won the election over Vice President Al Gore. Though Gore had won the popular vote nationally, the U. S. Supreme Court ordered (by a 5-4 vote) that the Florida recount be stopped and that Bush be awarded Florida's electoral votes. Bush won re-election in 2004, besting Senator John Kerry of Massachusetts. As President Bush has often said, his reputation will be determined in the future, not in

First Lady, Laura Lane Welch Bush, 1946–.

the present. He has said that history will prove that his response to the terrorist attacks of September 11, 2001 was justified. In that response, the President first ordered attacks on the Taliban government of Afghanistan. Next, and more significantly, the President made war on the government of President Saddam Hussein of Iraq, invading that country

As Director of Communications Dan Bartlett points to news footage of the World Trade Center Towers burning, President George W. Bush gathers information about the attack at Emma E. Booker Elementary School in Sarasota, Fla., Sept. 11, 2001.

in early 2003. Initially, a majority of Americans supported the invasion and war. As the war and its costs dragged on, most Americans came to believe that the war was a mistake, that the Bush government had misled the American people. President Bush's popularity has remained quite low since the 2004 election. Only roughly a third of Americans approve of the job he is doing as President. No one yet knows for sure what History will say about his presidency.

Spending Thanksgiving with some of the troops serving in Iraq, President Bush greets his fellow diners in the Bob Hope Dining Facility in Baghdad Nov. 27, 2003.

Barack Obama
(1961–)

★ **Forty-fourth President (2009–)** ★

WHEN HE TOOK OFFICE ON JANUARY 20TH, 2009 at age 47, President Obama was the fifth-youngest person ever to win the presidency. Only Grant, Theodore Roosevelt, Kennedy and Clinton (all in their forties) were younger. More noteworthy than his youth is the fact that he was the first person of color to be elected to the nation's highest office. Until four years before he was elected, he was almost unknown outside Chicago. Then, at the Democratic National Convention in 2004, he gave a stunning keynote speech which made him well-known nationally. He was elected U.S. Senator from Illinois that fall. His road to the nomination as the Democratic candidate for President in 2008 was extremely difficult. Many Democrats tried for the position, and his leading

First Lady, Michelle LaVaughn Obama, 1964–.

Barack Obama rose to national prominence through a stirring keynote speech at the 2004 Democratic Convention.

competitor, Senator Hillary Rodham Clinton of New York, was very powerful and popular among Democrats. Her husband, former President Bill Clinton, frequently spoke for her on the campaign trail, and many observers believed that Obama could not win against her. As the long primary season drew to a close in June, Obama had won a majority of his party's delegates, and Senator Clinton admitted defeat. In the fall campaign, Obama successfully identified his opponent, Senator John McCain of Arizona, with the presidency of George W. Bush. Because of Bush's record-breaking unpopularity, this technique worked with the voting public. Moreover, Obama argued that the war in Iraq, which McCain supported, had been a mistake from the beginning and that America should withdraw her troops as quickly as possible. He promised that no U.S. combat forces would remain in that country more than sixteen months into his presidency. Politically liberal, Obama also won the presidency because he demonstrated that much of America's economic suffering had come directly out of Republican deregulation of the financial services industries. When the votes were counted, Obama had earned 365 electoral votes and 53% of the popular vote against 173 and 46% for Senator McCain. It can safely be said that President Obama faces problems as great as any faced by Abraham Lincoln, who took office in 1861 on the eve of the Civil War, or by Franklin Roosevelt, who entered the Oval Office in 1933 during the fourth year of the Great Depression.

Obama's political career began as a community organizer on the streets of Chicago.

★ Illustration Sources ★

Page	Credit / Source
1	Seal of the President of the United States, Library of the Executive Office of the President.
25	White House, © James Steidl, 2007. Usage licensed through iStockphoto.
26	13-star Colonial U.S flag, public domain image.
26	Flag of the United States, public domain image.
27	Martha Washington, Library of Congress, lithograph by G.F. Gilman, c. 1876.
27	George Washington, Library of Congress, lithograph by G.F. Gilman, c. 1876.
28	"Washington Crossing the Delaware," painting by Emanuel Leutze, 1851, Metropolitan Museum of Art, New York City.
28	Mount Vernon, Library of Congress, lithograph, 1867.
29	John Adams, Library of Congress, painting by Gilbert Stuart.
29	Abigail Adams, Library of Congress, painting by Gilbert Stuart.
30	Writing the Declaration of Independence, Library of Congress, painting by Jean Leon Gerome.
30	John Adams 2-cent stamp, U.S. Postal Service.
31	Thomas Jefferson, Library of Congress, engraving.
31	Thomas Jefferson, full-length portrait, Library of Congress, engraving by Cornelius Tiebout, c. 1801.
32	Louisiana Purchase Treaty, U.S. National Archives.
32	Monticello, Library of Congress, illustration in *Century* magazine, May 1887.
33	James Madison, Library of Congress, illustration published by Pendleton's Lithography, c. 1828.
33	Dolley Madison, Library of Congress, Gilbert Stuart, published between 1804 and 1855.
34	The Battle of New Orleans, Library of Congress, painting by E. Percy Moran (1862–1935).
35	James Monroe, Library of Congress, illustration published by Pendleton's Lithography, c. 1828.
35	Missouri Compromise, U.S. National Archives.
36	Monroe Doctrine, U.S. National Archives.
37	John Q. Adams, Library of Congress, lithograph by Albert Newsam, published by C.S. Williams, c. 1846.
38	Andrew Jackson, Library of Congress, chromolithograph published between 1850 and 1900.
38	Mrs. Andrew Jackson, Library of Congress, engraving by John Chester Buttre, published by Bradley, Garretson & Co., 1883.
39	Jackson at Battle of New Orleans, Library of Congress, lithograph by Charles Severin, c. 1856.
39	Andrew Jackson Coin, 2007 Presidential $1 Coin image from the United States Mint.
40	Martin Van Buren, Library of Congress, lithograph by N. Currier, published between 1835 and 1856.
41	Wm. H. Harrison, Library of Congress, lithograph by Peter S. Duval, published by C.S. Williams, c. 1846.
41	Mrs. William Henry Harrison, Library of Congress, watercolor created between 1810–1870.
42	John Tyler, Library of Congress, lithograph by N. Currier, published between 1835 and 1856.
43	James K. Polk, Library of Congress, lithograph by Peter S. Duval, published by C.S. Williams, c. 1846.
43	Mrs. J.K. Polk, Library of Congress, lithograph by N. Currier, published 1846.
44	Zachary Taylor, Library of Congress, lithograph by N. Currier, published 1848.
44	Major General Taylor, Library of Congress, lithograph by N. Currier, published c. 1847.
45	Taylor at Battle of Buena Vista, Library of Congress, lithograph by N. Currier, published c. 1847.
46	Millard Fillmore, Library of Congress, lithograph by N. Currier, published c. 1848.
46	A slave auction in the south, Library of Congress, sketch by Theodore R. Davis 1861, published in: *Harper's Weekly*, 1861.
47	Compromise of 1850, U.S. National Archives.
48	Franklin Pierce, Library of Congress, lithograph by N. Currier, published c. 1852.
48	Mrs. Franklin Pierce, Library of Congress, engraving by John Chester Buttre, published by Funk & Wagnalls, 1886.
49	The "mustang" team, Library of Congress, lithograph of cartoon probably drawn by Louis Maurer, 1856.
50	James Buchanan, Library of Congress, lithograph by N. Currier, published between 1835 and 1856.
51	Dred Scott, Library of Congress, wood engraving published in *Century Magazine*, 1887.
51	Visit to Dred Scott—his family, Library of Congress, wood engravings after photoprints by Fitzgibbon, published in *Frank Leslie's Illustrated Newspaper*, June 27, 1857.
52	Abraham Lincoln, Library of Congress, photo by Alexander Gardner, February 5, 1865.
52	Mrs. Lincoln, Library of Congress, photo between 1855 and 1865.
53	Emancipation Proclamation, U.S. National Archives.
53	The Battle of Gettysburg, Library of Congress, lithograph by Currier & Ives, published c. 1863.
54	Gettysburg Address, U.S. National Archives.
54	President's box at Ford's Theatre, Library of Congress, photo April 1865.
54	John Wilkes Booth, Library of Congress, photo between 1860 and 1865.
55	Andrew Johnson, Library of Congress, lithograph by Bingham & Dodd, published c. 1866.
55	Mrs. Andrew Johnson, Library of Congress, engraving by John Chester Buttre, published by Bradley, Garretson & Co., 1883.
56	The man with the (carpet) bags, Library of Congress, wood engraving by Thomas Nast, published in *Harper's Weekly*, November 9, 1872.
56	The Senate as court of impeachment, Library of Congress, wood engraving by Theodore R. Davis, published in *Harper's Weekly*, April 11, 1868.
57	Ulysses S. Grant, Library of Congress, lithograph, probably created by Dominique C. Fabronius and published by Strobridge Lithographing Co., 1860s.
57	Mrs. Ulysses S. Grant, Library of Congress, photo between 1865 and 1885.
58	Ulysses S. Grant, Library of Congress, lithograph by Currier & Ives, published between 1856 and 1907.
58	Lincoln at Grant's headquarters, Library of Congress, lithograph by Currier & Ives, published c. 1865.
59	Rutherford B. Hayes, Library of Congress, chromolithograph by G. F. Gilman, c. 1877.
59	Mrs. Hayes, Library of Congress, photo by Charles Milton Bell, c. May 17, 1877.
60	Hayes Inauguration, Library of Congress, photo by Brady National Photographic Art Gallery, 1877.
61	James A. Garfield, Library of Congress, photo, between 1870 and 1881.
61	Mrs. Garfield, Library of Congress, photo, between 1860 and 1870.
62	Gen. Garfield, Library of Congress, lithograph by Kurz & Allison, published c, Jan 6, 1882.
62	The attack on Garfield 's life, Library of Congress, wood engraving by A. Berghaus & C. Upham, published in *Frank Leslie's Illustrated Newspaper*, July 16, 1881.
63	Chester Arthur, Library of Congress, photo by Charles Milton Bell, 1882.
63	Mrs. Chester Arthur, Library of Congress, photo between 1857 and 1870.
64	Judge Brady administering oath, Library of Congress, wood engraving, published in *Frank Leslie's Illustrated Newspaper*, Oct. 8, 1881.
64	President Arthur crossing Brooklyn Bridge, Library of Congress, wood engraving, published in *Harper's Weekly*, June 2, 1883.
65	Grover Cleveland, Library of Congress, photo by N. Sarony, c. 1892.
65	Mrs. Cleveland, Library of Congress, photo c. Jul. 25, 1888.
66	Haymarket Riot, Library of Congress, wood engraving, drawn by T. de Thulstrup from sketches and photos furnished by H. Jeaneret, published in *Harper's Weekly*, May 15, 1886.
66	Inauguration of Bartholdi Statue, Library of Congress, photo copyright H. O'Neil, c. Oct. 28, 1886.
67	Benjamin Harrison, Library of Congress, photo copyright Pach Brothers, c. 1896.
67	Mrs. Harrison, Library of Congress, photo copyright Charles Parker, c. Jul. 9, 1889.
68	General Harrison, Library of Congress, lithograph by Kurz & Allison, published c. 1888.
68	Caricature of Harrison, Library of Congress, lithograph by Joseph Ferdinand Keppler, published in *Puck*, Aug. 13, 1890.
69	William C. McKinley, Library of Congress, photo c. 1900.
69	Mrs. McKinley, Library of Congress, photo c. May 23, 1900.
70	McKinley cartoon, Library of Congress, lithograph by Grant E. Hamilton, published in *Judge*, Feb. 4, 1899.
70	Assassination of President McKinley, Library of Congress, wash drawing by T. Dart Walker, published c.1905.

71 Theodore Roosevelt, Library of Congress, photo, copyright Pach Bros., c. 1904.

71 Mrs. Roosevelt, Library of Congress, Brady-Handy Photograph Collection, photo between 1890 and 1910.

72 Theodore Roosevelt rough rider, Library of Congress, photo c. Oct. 26, 1898.

72 Roosevelt during construction of Panama Canal, Library of Congress, photo, copyright H.C. White Co., c. 1908.

73 William Howard Taft, Library of Congress, chromolithograph, published by Allied Printing Trades Council, c. 1908.

73 Mrs. Taft, Library of Congress, photo, published by Bain News Service c. 1910.

74 Judge speaks, Library of Congress, lithograph by Eugene Zimmerman, published in *Judge*, Oct. 30, 1909.

74 Supreme Court Justices of 1925, U.S. Government photo, 1925.

75 Woodrow Wilson, Library of Congress, photo, copyright Pach Bros., c. Dec. 2, 1912.

75 Mrs. Wilson, Library of Congress, photo, published by Bain News Service c. 1915.

76 Red Cross poster, Library of Congress, lithograph by Harrison Fisher, published by the American Red Cross, 1918.

76 Woodrow Wilson asking Congress to declare war, Library of Congress, print, Apr. 2, 1917.

77 Warren G. Harding, Library of Congress, photo, copyright by Moffett, c. June 21, 1920.

77 Mrs. Harding, Library of Congress, photo, copyright Underwood & Underwood Studios, between 1920 and 1923.

78 Warren G. Harding & Gen. Pershing, Library of Congress, photo, published by Bain News Service c. 1922.

78 Funeral cortege for President Harding, Library of Congress, photo, National Photo Company Collection, August 8, 1923.

79 Calvin Coolidge, Library of Congress, photo by Notman Photo Co., c. 1919.

79 Mrs. Coolidge, Library of Congress, photo, copyright Harris & Ewing, c. Jan. 2, 1924.

80 Picketing the White House, Library of Congress, photo, National Photo Company Collection, April 15, 1926.

80 Lindbergh and mother with President and Mrs. Coolidge, Library of Congress, National Photo Company Collection, photo June 12, 1927.

80 Lindbergh with Spirit of St. Louis, Library of Congress, photo c. 1927.

81 Herbert Hoover, Library of Congress, photo, copyright Underwood & Underwood, c. 1928.

81 Mrs. Hoover, Library of Congress, Gottscho-Schleisner Collection, photo by Samuel Herman Gottscho, Mar. 10, 1933.

82 Impoverished family on New Mexico highway, Library of Congress, photo by Dorothea Lange, Farm Security Administration, Aug. 1936.

82 Houston St., N.Y.C. Junk markets, Library of Congress, Gottscho-Schleisner Collection, photo by Samuel H. Gottscho, March 10, 1933.

82 Squatters' shacks, Library of Congress, photo by Arthur Rothstein, Farm Security Administration, July 1936.

83 Franklin Delano Roosevelt, Library of Congress, photo by Elias Goldensky, c. Dec 27, 1933.

83 Mrs. Roosevelt, Library of Congress, photo c. July 20, 1933.

84 WPA Rumor Poster, Library of Congress, by Vera Bock, Federal Art Project, between 1939 – 1941.

84 Poster promoting the U.S. Civilian Conservation Corps, Library of Congress, by Albert M. Bender, Illinois WPA Art Project, 1941.

84 Social Security Poster, Franklin D. Roosevelt Library, published by U.S. Social Security Admin.

84 Pearl Harbor, Library of Congress, photo by U.S. Navy, Office of Public Relations, Dec. 1941.

85 Roosevelt signing declaration of war, Library of Congress, Office of War Information photo Dec, 1941.

85 Crimean Conference, Library of Congress, collections of Encyclopedia Britannica, photo February 1945.

85 Roosevelt's funeral procession, Library of Congress, photo c. Apr. 24, 1945.

86 Harry S. Truman, Harry S. Truman Presidential Library, photo c. 1947.

86 Mrs. Truman, Library of Congress, photo by Harris & Ewing between 1944 and 1953.

87 Atomic Bomb, Library of Congress, U.S. Army Air Force photo, Aug. 1945.

87 Douglas MacArthur in Korea, Library of Congress, photo by USASC, Jan. 28,1951.

88 Dwight Eisenhower, Eisenhower Presidential Library, photo Feb. 13, 1959.

88 Mamie Eisenhower, Eisenhower Presidential Library, photo May 23, 1956.

89 ICBM, USAF photo.

89 Khruschev examines wreckage, Eisenhower Presidential Library, photo.

89 U2 spy plane, USAF photo.

90 President John F. Kennedy, John F. Kennedy Presidential Library, photo by Cecil Stoughton, July 1963.

90 Mrs. Kennedy, John F. Kennedy Presidential Library, photo by Robert Knudsen, May 22, 1962.

91 March on Washington, Library of Congress, U.S. News & World Report Magazine Photograph Collection, photo by Warren K. Leffler, Aug. 28, 1963.

91 President meets with the leaders of the march, photo by Cecil Stoughton, White House/John Fitzgerald Kennedy Library, Boston. Aug. 28, 1963.

91 President Kennedy inspects "Friendship 7," photo by Cecil Stoughton, White House/John F. Kennedy Presidential Library, Boston. Feb. 23, 1962.

91 "Freedom 7" launch, NASA photo May 5, 1961.

92 U2 Image, CIA photo Oct. 1962

92 Stevenson shows photos at UN, United Nations Photo Library, photo Nov. 1962.

92 Kennedy motorcade, Library of Congress, photo by Victor Hugo King, Nov. 22, 1963.

92 Mrs. Kennedy and children leave Capitol, John F. Kennedy Presidential Library, photo by Abbie Rowe, National Park Service. Nov. 4, 1963.

92 Procession to St. Matthew's Cathedral, John F. Kennedy Presidential Library, photo by Abbie Rowe, National Park Service. Nov. 25, 1963

93 Lyndon B. Johnson, LBJ Library, photo by Yoichi R. Okamoto, Jan. 9, 1969.

93 "Lady Bird" Johnson, LBJ Library, photo by Robert Knudsen, Oct. 20, 1967.

94 Swearing in of Lyndon B. Johnson, LBJ Library, photo by Cecil Stoughton, Nov. 22, 1963.

94 Johnson signs 1968 Civil Rights Bill, Library of Congress, U.S. News & World Report Magazine Photograph Collection, photo by Warren K. Leffler, April 11, 1968.

94 Johnson with Dr. King, LBJ Library, photo by Yoichi R. Okamoto, March 18, 1966.

94 Anti-war protest, LBJ Library, photo by Robert Knudsen, May 17, 1967.

95 Richard M. Nixon, Nixon Library, photo July 9, 1972.

95 Pat Nixon, Nixon Library, photo Feb. 21, 1973.

96 Nixon at Great Wall, Nixon Library, photo Feb. 24, 1972.

96 Nixon resignation, U.S. National Archives, August 9, 1974.

97 Gerald R. Ford, Gerald R. Ford Library, White House photo by David Hume Kennerly, Aug. 27, 1974.

97 Mrs. Ford, Library of Congress, White House photo, 1974.

98 Announcing pardon, courtesy Gerald R. Ford Library, photo Sep. 8, 1974.

98 Helicopters landing, U.S. Military photo, April 1975.

98 Pushing helicopter overboard, U.S. Military photo, April 1975.

99 Jimmy Carter, Library of Congress, White House photo, Jan. 31, 1977.

99 Mrs. Carter, Library of Congress, White House photo, Feb. 18, 1977.

100 Camp David, Jimmy Carter Library, White House photo, Sept. 7, 1978.

100 Nobel Peace Prize, The Carter Center, courtesy of Knudsen Photos, Dec. 10, 2002.

101 Ronald Reagan, Ronald Reagan Library, White House photo, 1981.

101 Nancy Reagan, Ronald Reagan Library, White House photo, Feb. 1, 1983.

102 Reagan assassination, Ronald Reagan Library, photos March 3, 1981.

102 Space shuttle Challenger, NASA photos, Jan. 28, 1986.

103 Reagan & Gorbachev signing INF Treaty, Ronald Reagan Library, photo Dec. 8, 1987.

103 Reagan & Gorbachev standing, Geneva Summit, Ronald Reagan Library, photo Nov. 19, 1985.

103 Receiving Tower Commission Report, Ronald Reagan Library, photo Feb. 26, 1987.

104 George H.W. Bush, George Bush Presidential Library, White House photo, Feb. 15, 1989.

104 Barbara Bush, George Bush Presidential Library, photo 1999.

105 Gulf War, George Bush Presidential Library, photo Nov. 22, 1990.

105 With Emir of Kuwait, George Bush Presidential Library, photo Sept. 9, 1990.

106 Bill Clinton, White House photo, Jan. 1, 1993.

106 Hillary Clinton, U.S. Senate photo.

107 At signing of Dayton–Paris Accord, U.S. Government photo, Dec. 1. 1995.

107 Clinton in Bosnia, Clinton Presidential Library, White House Photo Office, Jan 13, 1996.

107 Clinton and the 2000 Budget, Clinton Presidential Library, White House Photo Office, Feb. 1, 1999.

108 George W. Bush, White House photo, 2003.

108 Laura Bush, White House photo.

109 Bush in FL, 9/11, White House photo by Eric Draper, Sept. 11, 2001.

109 Thanksgiving troops in Iraq, White House photo by Tina Hager, Nov. 27, 2003.

110 Barack Obama, U.S. Senate photo.

110 Michelle Obama, Obama campaign press photo.

111 Obama at 2004 DNC, Kerry campaign press photo.

111 Community organizer, Obama campaign press photo.

★ About the Authors ★

Valden Madsen has been interested in the American presidency for most of his life. At the University of Wisconsin, where he earned his bachelor's degree, he minored in History and American Studies before going on to earn graduate degrees in literature and writing. Intriguing to him are the fascinating parallels as well as the differences between the monarchies of Europe and the democratic-republican tradition within which the U.S. presidency developed. Some Presidents have been every bit as kingly as European kings ever were; many have been more or less ordinary folks.

A resident of Manhattan and New York State's Hudson River Valley, Valden Madsen is rarely far away from presidential history. In New York City he lives one block away from Cooper Union's Great Hall, the location of Abraham Lincoln's famous 1860 speech, the one that made him nationally known when New York City's newspaper editors spread the word about his skills and intelligence. Madsen's farm in Hudson, New York, is just twenty minutes south of Kinderhook, where President Martin Van Buren was born and is buried, and forty minutes south of Albany, where Presidents Theodore and Franklin Delano Roosevelt both served as Governors of the State of New York. Also, on a less famous note, the tomb of President Chester Alan Arthur is in Albany.

Lucas Alikani Cohen and his parents and sister divide their time between an apartment on Manhattan's Upper West Side and a farm in New York's Hudson River Valley. In New York City, Lucas lives just a mile or so south of the tomb where President Ulysses S. Grant and his wife are buried. In the country, his family and he live thirty minutes north of Hyde Park, the location of Franklin Delano Roosevelt's home, Presidential library and burial site. In addition to the Presidents of the United States, Lucas is interested in paleontology and fresh-water biology, among other studies. In the fall of 2009, he will begin the eighth grade at the Calhoun School in Manhattan.

George Washington

John Adams

Thomas Jefferson

James Madison

James Monroe

John Quincy Adams

Andrew Jackson

Martin Van Buren

William Henry Harrison

Thomas Jefferson
(1743-1826)
Third President (1801-1809):

"One man with courage is a majority."

1. Like most southern aristocrats, including most U.S. presidents elected from the South up until the Civil War, Jefferson was a slaveholder.

2. Four of his six children died in infancy.

3. Literate in classical Greek, he edited his own version of the New Testament.

4. A believer in freedom of thought, Jefferson was the sworn enemy of what he called "every form of tyranny over the mind of man."

5. John Adams and he were bitter political enemies, but later became close friends.

6. He had no constitutional authority for making the Lousiana Purchase of 1803, which doubled the size of the United States. His action was probably an abuse of presidential power.

John Adams
(1735-1826)
Second President (1797-1801):

"The happiness of society is the purpose of government."

1. He was the first President to live in the White House. He spent the last several months of his presidency in the new mansion.

2. His wife, Abigail, was one of the first Americans who thought women might someday become citizens with civil rights.

3. His exchange of letters with Thomas Jefferson is a valuable series of history lessons.

4. Asked to write the Declaration of Independence, he insisted that Jefferson do so, believing him a better writer.

5. His son, John Quincy Adams, became the Sixth President, and many of his other descendants achieved fame as authors and politicians.

6. He was one of only three Presidents to live beyond his 90th birthday: Gerald Ford and Ronald Reagan were the others.

George Washington
(1732-1799)
First President (1789-1797):

"Liberty, when it begins to take root, is a plant of rapid growth."

1. Although he is the Father of his Country, he had no children.

2. During his service in the British army against the French, four bullets pierced his coat without injuring him.

3. Although trained by the British General Edward Braddock, he later used his skills to lead American troops against the British.

4. He refused to accept the presidential salary of $25,000 a year.

5. In his farewell address (September, 1796), he cautioned his country against getting involved in the affairs of other nations.

6. His false teeth, which didn't fit very well, were made of animal bone, ivory, and other materials, not of wood as is usually thought.

John Quincy Adams
(1767-1848)
Sixth President (1825-1829):

"America does not go abroad in search of monsters to destroy."

1. As a boy, he watched the Revolutionary War Battle of Bunker Hill from a hill on his family's farm in Quincy, Massachusetts.

2. In the election of 1824, neither Adams nor any of his competitors received a majority of electoral votes. The election was decided in Adams's favor by the U. S. House of Representatives.

3. Andrew Jackson, who won many more popular votes than Adams did in 1824, immediately began plotting against him.

4. His third son, Charles Francis Adams, became a U. S. ambassador who kept the French and British from openly siding with the Confederate States during the American Civil War.

5. His oldest son, George Washington Adams, suffered from the disease of alcoholism, and died at age 28, an apparent suicide.

James Monroe
(1758-1831)
Fifth President (1817-1825):

"A little flattery will support a man through great fatigue."

1. Jefferson said, "Monroe was so honest that if you turned his soul inside out there would not be a spot on it."

2. The Monroe Doctrine, which said that European powers were no longer free to colonize North or South America, did not earn its name until the 1850s, twenty years after Monroe's death.

3. Spain gave up its rights to Florida to the United States in 1821, right after Monroe's re-election.

4. Monrovia, the capital of the African country of Liberia, is named after President Monroe because freed American slaves settled there.

5. In 1820 he won all but one of the votes of the electoral college. He would have been given all of them, but the Electors wanted only Washington to be remembered in that way.

James Madison
(1751-1836)
Fourth President (1809-1817):

"The truth is that all men having power ought to be mistrusted."

1. He was so busy with politics that he didn't marry until 1794, at the age of 43.

2. He was one of six presidents who had no children. (The others were Washington, Jackson, Polk, Buchanan, and Harding.)

3. A very close ally of both Jefferson and Washington, Madison was an essential figure at the Constitutional Convention of 1787.

4. As President, he allowed himself to be talked into the disastrous war of 1812 against Great Britain.

5. Madison was the smallest of the Presidents, weighing only about 100 pounds and standing only 5'4" tall.

6. Madison's political party, the Democratic-Republican, was the only significant one in America from 1812 until the Whigs appeared in the early 1840s.

William Henry Harrison
(1773-1841)
Ninth President (March-April 1841):

"The strongest of all governments is that which is most free."

1. The first President to die in office, Harrison also served the shortest term: only one month, from March 4th to April 4th, 1841.

2. Born a wealthy Virginian, he spent most of his adult life in Indiana and other territories far from Virginia.

3. He led armies against the great Indian warrior-chief, Tecumseh.

4. Totally inexperienced as a politician, Harrison was elected President because of his reputation as a war hero.

5. He was the grandfather of another President, Benjamin Harrison.

Martin Van Buren
(1782-1862)
Eighth President (1837-1841):

"As to the Presidency, the two happiest days of my life were those of my entrance upon the office and my surrender of it."

1. Of Dutch descent and a life-long resident of New York's Hudson River Valley, he was born and raised in Kinderhook, New York.

2. He opposed adding Texas to the United States because he feared the addition of more slave-holding states to the Union.

3. He was known as "The Little Magician" because of his ability to win votes.

4. Van Buren ordered the tragic removal of the Indians of the Cherokee Nation from Georgia to Oklahoma in 1838-39.

5. In 1840, President Van Buren opposed the American abolitionists who wanted to free the slaves of the ship Amistad.

6. Later in life he became extremely conservative in his politics.

Andrew Jackson
(1767-1845)
Seventh President (1829-1837):

"I can command [an army] but I am not fit to be President."

1. Although he was successful as a lawyer, he had no formal education.

2. An enemy of his said something nasty about Jackson's wife, and Jackson killed the man in a duel.

3. He was the first member of the House of Representatives from the new state of Tennessee and later served as one of its senators.

4. As President he seemed so much like a dictator to his enemies that hostile cartoonists referred to him as "King Andrew."

5. To his friends—but not in public—he threatened to hang John Calhoun, one of his political enemies.

6. He was the first ordinary person to become President, and was wildly popular among regular citizens, but not among the wealthy.

John Tyler

James Polk

Zachary Taylor

Millard Fillmore

Franklin Pierce

James Buchanan

Abraham Lincoln

Andrew Johnson

Ulysses S. Grant

Zachary Taylor
(1784-1850)
Twelfth President (1849-1850):

"The idea that I should become President . . . has never entered my head, nor is it likely to enter the head of any other person."

1. Like William Henry Harrison, Zachary Taylor had had no experience as a politician before becoming President. Also like Harrison, Taylor died early in his presidential term.

2. His daughter, Sarah, was the first wife of Jefferson Davis, who later became President of the Confederate States of America.

3. In response to southern politicians threatening to withdraw their states from the Union, Taylor roared that they would be hanged as he had hanged deserters and spies during the war with Mexico.

4. He was a much more successful general than he was a President, though he might have done good things had he lived longer.

James Polk
(1795-1849)
Eleventh President (1845-1849):

"With me it is exceptionally true that the Presidency is no bed of roses."

1. During his administration more territory was added to the United States (from lands taken from Mexico in the Southwest) than at any time since Jefferson's Lousiana Purchase in 1803.

2. Andrew Jackson, old but powerful, supported Polk's efforts to become President.

3. Because he was allied with former President Jackson (well-known for his toughness as "Old Hickory"), Polk was sometimes called "Young Hickory."

4. Polk's war against Mexico was the first unpopular war America fought. Henry David Thoreau went to jail rather than pay the tax which funded it.

5. Many Americans came to believe that it was their "Manifest [obvious] Destiny" to own and govern most of North America.

John Tyler
(1790-1862)
Tenth President (1841-1845):

"Here lies the body of my good horse, 'The General.' For twenty years . . . he never made a blunder. Would that his master could say the same!"

1. He was the first Vice President to become President upon the death of the President, in this case William Henry Harrison.

2. Because he was not elected President, his enemies called him "His Accidency."

3. He had the most children of any President: fifteen, by two wives.

4. He was a member of the U. S. House of Representatives, Governor of Virginia, and a U. S. Senator from Virginia before becoming Vice President and then President.

5. During the first years of the Civil War, 1861-62, he was a member of the Confederate States Congress.

James Buchanan
(1791-1868)
Fifteenth President (1857-1861):

"There is nothing stable but Heaven and the Constitution."

1 He was the only President who never married.

2. His niece, Harriet Lane, served as his White House hostess.

3. Earlier in his career, he served as Minister to the imperial court of Russia.

4. He wanted Kansas admitted to the union as a state where slavery would be legal.

5. As southern states began to leave the Union before the Civil War began, he denied that they had the legal right to do so. At the same time, he did not believe the federal government could legally prevent them from withdrawing.

Franklin Pierce
(1804-1869)
Fourteenth President (1853-1857):

"Americans have nothing in their history or position to invite aggression."

1. A New Hampshireman, he was the first New Englander to win the presidency since John Quincy Adams was elected in 1824.

2. He was elected to the New Hampshire legislature at age 24.

3. First as a representative, then as a senator, he served the people of New Hampshire in Washington.

4. When the Democrats nominated him in 1852, few people knew who he was: the delegates couldn't agree on any of the better-known candidates.

5. After his election, but before he took office, Pierce's only surviving child was killed in a train crash at the age of eleven.

6. He authorized the Gadsden Purchase, which bought parts of southern New Mexico and Arizona from Mexico.

Millard Fillmore
(1800-1874)
Thirteenth President (1850-1853):

"An honorable defeat is better than a dishonorable victory."

1. Born in 1800 in the Finger Lakes region of New York State, he was a true child of the frontier.

2. After informally studying law, he began to practice that profession in Buffalo, New York at the age of 30.

3. He served in the U. S. House of Representatives and became Vice President when Zachary Taylor was elected. He became President when Taylor died in office.

4. He signed the Fugitive Slave Act which required northerners to return escaped slaves to their southern owners.

5. California was admitted to the Union as a state where slavery was illegal.

Ulysses S. Grant
(1822-1885)
Eighteenth President (1869-1877):

"I have never advocated war except as a means of peace."

1. He was born in Ohio, lived in Illinois and died in New York. His and his wife's tomb on Riverside Drive in New York City is still a popular tourist destination.

2. During his second term, the presidential salary was increased from $25,000 to $50,000. This was the first raise a President had received since the birth of the country.

3. All four of his children lived to older adulthood, dying between the ages of 62 and 77. This was a small miracle in an age when so many children died in infancy or childhood.

4. Bankrupt and dying of throat cancer, he struggled to complete his memoirs. After his death his book earned more than $450,000, millions of dollars in Twenty-first Century money.

Andrew Johnson
(1808-1875)
Seventeenth President (1865-1869):

"Honest conviction is my courage; the Constitution is my guide."

1. Johnson was Lincoln's second Vice President, beginning his service in that office only about one month before Lincoln's assassination.

2. Although he was the Republican Lincoln's Vice President, Johnson was a member of the Democratic party.

3. He believed strongly in the rights of the individual states, but remained in the U. S. Senate when his state, Tennessee, withdrew from the Union prior to the Civil War.

4. He was impeached by the House of Representatives in 1867; the Senate failed by just one vote to convict him.

5. He served as President until 1869, then retired for several years before returning to Washington as a senator in 1875, a few months before his death.

Abraham Lincoln
(1809-1865)
Sixteenth President (1861-1865):

"If slavery is not wrong, nothing is wrong."

1. He actually lived in several different log cabins when he was a child and young man.

2. Self-taught, he modeled his excellent writing style on Shakespeare and on the 1611 King James translation of the Bible.

3. His only national political experience before becoming President was two years in the U. S. House of Representatives.

4. Everyone thinks of him as "Honest Abe," but he denied many American citizens their basic rights during the Civil War.

5. His wife was a southerner; many of her relatives fought in the Confederate States army.

6. Three of his four sons died before reaching maturity, one of them during Lincoln's presidency.

Rutherford B. Hayes

James A. Garfield

Chester Alan Arthur

Grover Cleveland

Benjamin Harrison

William McKinley

Theodore Roosevelt

William Howard Taft

Woodrow Wilson

Chester Alan Arthur
(1830-1886)
Twenty-first President (1881-1885):

*"If it were not for the reporters,
I would tell you the truth."*

1. He never held an elected office until he became President Garfield's Vice President in 1881.

2. He was known as "Elegant Arthur" because of his luxuriant whiskers and fondness for fashionable clothes.

3. During his administration, the Civil Service Commission was established.

4. The first Federal immigration law was passed during his administration. It excluded poor people, criminals and those suffering from mental illness from entering the United States.

5. Chinese immigration into the U. S. was suspended for ten years, the restriction later becoming permanent. This discriminatory ruling remained in place until 1965.

James A. Garfield
(1831-1881)
Twentieth President (1881):

*"I have had many troubles in my life,
but the worst of them never came."*

1. Born in Ohio, Garfield attended Williams College in Massachusetts.

2. He was later a professor of classics and president of Hiram College in Ohio.

3. He was a major general in the Union Army. Lincoln persuaded him to give up his command and enter Congress as a Republican.

4. He served eighteen years in Congress.

5. He was assassinated during his first year as President.

Rutherford B. Hayes
(1822-1893)
Nineteenth President (1877-1881):

*"Nothing brings out the lower traits of
human nature like office seeking."*

1. He rose to the rank of Major General in the Union army.

2. He was elected to the U. S. House of Representatives while still on active duty in the army.

3. His wife was known as "Lemonade Lucy" because she did not allow wine or other alcoholic beverages in the White House.

4. He withdrew U. S. troops from the South, which permitted white politicians to discriminate against former slaves.

5. He was the first President to use a telephone in the White House.

6. He had promised to serve only one term as President, and kept his word, declining to run for re-election.

William McKinley
(1843-1901)
Twenty-fifth President (1897-1901):

*"In the time of darkest defeat,
victory may be nearest."*

1. He enlisted as a private in the Union army during the Civil War and rose to the rank of major.

2. An Ohioan, he attended Allegheny College briefly and taught school.

3. He began his career in government as a member of the U. S. House of Representatives in 1876.

4. He left the House after fourteen years to become Governor of Ohio.

5. Elected to the presidency in 1896, he and the country enjoyed the prosperity that followed the end of the Depression of 1893.

6. He was assassinated in 1901, early in his second term, at the Buffalo, New York Pan-American Exposition.

Benjamin Harrison
(1833-1901)
Twenty-third President (1889-1893):

*"We Americans have no commission
from God to police the world."*

1. The grandson of President William Henry Harrison, he was born in Ohio but moved to Indiana early in his life.

2. He was a Colonel in the Civil War.

3. In his career as a Senator, he earned the criticism of his enemies by being kind to such people as Indians, poor farmers and Civil War veterans.

4. In the presidential election of 1888 he received 100,000 fewer popular votes than Cleveland did, but won the Electoral College 233 to 168.

5. Harrison wanted to make Hawaii part of the U. S., but before the Senate could act, Cleveland was elected President and withdrew the treaty from consideration.

Grover Cleveland
(1837-1908)
Twenty-second and Twenty-fourth Presidents (1885-1889, 1893-1897):

"Above all, tell the truth."

1. From boyhood, he was known by his middle name, Grover, not by his given name Stephen.

2. He is the only President to serve non-consecutive terms.

3. Like several other candidates, from Andrew Jackson in 1824 to Albert Gore in 2000, Cleveland won the popular vote but lost the electoral vote. Thus he lost the presidency in 1888.

4. He was a bachelor when he became President but married in June, 1886, early in his first term.

5. The Interstate Commerce Act, which became law during his administration, attempted to regulate the railroads.

6. The Depression of 1893 prevented the success of his second term.

Woodrow Wilson
(1856-1924)
Twenty-eighth President (1913-1921):

*"If you want to make enemies,
try to change something."*

1. Like Presidents Grover Cleveland and Calvin Coolidge, Wilson never used his first name, Thomas.

2. He saw the results of the Civil War: his father was a minister in Augusta, Georgia and a professor in Columbia, South Carolina.

3. He attended Princeton University and the University of Virginia School of Law; he earned his Ph.D. from Johns Hopkins.

4. He won the governorship of New Jersey in 1910 and the presidency of the United States in 1912.

5. He kept the U. S. out of World War I from 1914 until 1917.

6. When he finally took his country to war in 1917, he saw it as part of a worldwide effort "to keep the world safe for democracy."

William Howard Taft
(1857-1930)
Twenty-seventh President (1909-1913):

*"Politics, when I am in it,
makes me sick."*

1. He was the first President to enjoy the new pay raise, from $50,000 to $75,000 per year.

2. He was President McKinley's civilian administrator in the Philippines, where he was generally fair with the Filipinos.

3. As President Roosevelt's Secretary of War, he did such a good job that Roosevelt decided Taft would be the next President.

4. As President, Taft continued most of Roosevelt's policies at home and abroad.

5. Taft weighed more than 300 pounds.

6. He became a conservative Republican. This angered Roosevelt, who left the Republican party to run against him in 1912, thus ensuring that the Democrat, Woodrow Wilson, would win.

Theodore Roosevelt
(1858-1919)
Twenty-sixth President (1901-1909):

*"The only man who makes no mistake is
the man who does nothing."*

1. At 42, he was the youngest person ever to become president.

2. He had served as William McKinley's Vice President only briefly before becoming President in his own right.

3. He was an extremely fragile boy who took physical fitness very seriously. Living like a frontiersman in South Dakota, he always believed, made a man of him.

4. His mother and his first wife both died on the same day in 1884.

5. He won the Nobel Peace prize in 1906 for helping end the war between Japan and Russia.

6. One of his favorite sayings was, "Speak softly and carry a big stick."

★ Warren Harding

★ Calvin Coolidge

★ Herbert Hoover

★ Franklin Delano Roosevelt

★ Harry Truman

★ Dwight Eisenhower

★ John F. Kennedy

★ Lyndon Baines Johnson

★ Richard M. Nixon

Herbert Hoover
(1874-1964)
Thirty-first President (1929-1933):

"Freedom of the press to discuss public questions is a foundation of American liberty."

1. Hoover was one of the first students at Stanford University when it opened in 1891.
2. After graduating with a degree in engineering, he traveled to China with his wife to work for an American corporation.
3. Back in America, he and his wife spoke Chinese when they didn't want to be overheard.
4. After World War I ended, Hoover helped organize shipments of food for millions of starving Europeans.
5. He did a good job as Secretary of Commerce for Presidents Harding and Coolidge.
6. In his inaugural address in March of 1929, he predicted endless prosperity for America; in October of that year, the Great Depression began.

Calvin Coolidge
(1872-1933)
Thirtieth President (1923-1929):

"I have never been hurt by anything I didn't say."

1. Coolidge was a New Englander: born in Vermont, he lived in Massachusetts as an adult.
2. As he worked his way up through Massachusetts politics, he became an extremely conservative Republican.
3. He became President when Harding died in office, and set to work without wasting a minute.
4. He enjoyed what was known as "Coolidge prosperity," and was re-elected in 1924 with 54% of the popular vote.
5. Economic well-being continued during the rest of his second term, but when he left office, the Great Depression of 1929 was only seven months away.
6. He could easily have been re-elected in 1928, but chose not to run again.

Warren Harding
(1865-1923)
Twenty-ninth President (1921-1923):

"I have no trouble with my enemies . . . but my friends keep me walking the floor nights."

1. An Ohioan, Harding was a life-long Republican who did volunteer work for both parties during his younger years.
2. He was first elected to the Senate in 1914.
3. His presidential campaign promises in 1920 were so vague that no one knew whether he favored joining the League of Nations. (He wanted the U. S. to stay out of it.)
4. He won the Presidency by a landslide, 60% of the popular vote.
5. Although he and his wife had no children, he was probably the father of a baby born to Nan Britton in 1919.
6. The corruption of his administration did not become obvious until after his death.

Dwight Eisenhower
(1890-1969)
Thirty-fourth President (1953-1961):

"I never saw a pessimistic general win a battle."

1. Because he was born in Texas but brought up in Kansas, both states claim him as a native son.
2. Until he chose to run for President as a Republican in 1952, he had no political association.
3. In his presidency, the 20th Century African-American civil rights movement took its first serious steps forward.
4. He was the last President born in the 19th Century.
5. He was the most famous general elected to the presidency since Ulysses S. Grant's election in 1868.
6. His grandson, David Eisenhower, wrote an excellent biography of him many years after his grandfather's death.

Harry Truman
(1884-1972)
Thirty-third President (1945-1953):

"You cannot stop the spread of an idea by passing a law against it."

1. He first came to national attention by serving on the Senate committee responsible for saving billions of dollars in costs for World War II.
2. He said he felt like a load of hay had fallen on him when FDR died and he had to accept the burden of the presidency.
3. During his administration, the annual presidential salary was increased to $100,000, plus a $50,000 expense account.
4. He was elected in his own right in 1948, running against what he called the "do nothing" Republican Congress.
5. In accepting responsibility for his actions as President, he popularized the saying, "The buck stops here."
6. In July of 1945, he witnessed the founding of the United Nations.

Franklin Delano Roosevelt
(1882-1945)
Thirty-second President (1933-1945):

"The only thing we have to fear is fear itself."

1. As Presidents Coolidge and Hoover restored America's faith in the presidency, FDR's task was to restore America's faith in herself during the Great Depression.
2. Born into the Hudson River Valley's upper class, he entered politics as a Democrat, trying to help ordinary Americans.
3. After falling victim to polio at 39, he was never able to walk on his own again.
4. He was Commander-in-Chief of the armed forces through all but the final four months of World War II, 1941-1945.
5. He was the only President to be elected more than twice; he died less than three months into his fourth term.
6. He was the first President to be inaugurated on January 20th; all previous inaugurations had been held on the 4th of March.

Richard M. Nixon
(1913-1994)
Thirty-seventh President (1969-1974):

"Those who hate you don't win unless you hate them. And then you destroy yourself."

1. Nixon was a child of the Depression, born into a poor California family.
2. The televised 1960 presidential debates between John Kennedy and him proved vitally important to his losing that election.
3. When he lost his bid to become Governor of California in 1962, everyone assumed that he would disappear from public life. A decade after that, he was re-elected to the presidency by one of the greatest majorities in the history of presidential elections.
4. By the time he resigned the presidency in August of 1974, his approval rating had fallen to about 23%.
5. He is the only President ever to resign.
6. He was the first to enjoy the presidential salary increase from $100,000 to $200,000 per year.

Lyndon Baines Johnson
(1908-1973)
Thirty-sixth President (1963-1969):

" If government is to serve any purpose it is to do for others what they are unable to do for themselves."

1. LBJ was raised in rural Texas and became a teacher before running for election to the U. S. House of Representatives in 1937.
2. Johnson came into office under the cloud of John F. Kennedy's assassination.
3. Under Johnson, the U. S. Congress passed more civil rights legislation than had been passed in the previous century.
4. LBJ expanded the U. S. commitment in Vietnam. By the end of his presidency, more than a half million American service members were fighting there.
5. Johnson always wanted to be known as the President who did the most for education in what he called "the Great Society."

John F. Kennedy
(1917-1963)
Thirty-fifth President (1961-1963):

"Ask not what your country can do for you, ask what you can do for your country."

1. JFK served heroically in World War II, was seriously wounded and suffered throughout his life from pain resulting from his wounds.
2. While recovering from his war wounds, he wrote PROFILES IN COURAGE, which won the Pulitzer Prize in history.
3. He was the first Roman Catholic elected President.
4. He was the youngest man ever elected President, and also the youngest to die.
5. He married Jacqueline Bouvier in 1953. She and their children, John and Caroline, all became newsworthy Americans.
6. President Kennedy began involving America in the civil war in Vietnam to a meaningful degree.

Gerald Ford

Jimmy Carter

Ronald Reagan

George H. W. Bush

Bill Clinton

George W. Bush

Barack Obama

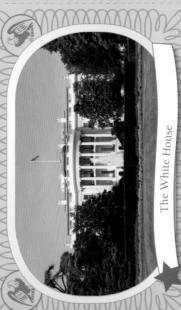

The White House

The Oval Office

Ronald Reagan
(1911-2004)
Fortieth President (1981-1989):
"America is too great for small dreams."

1. Born and raised in Illinois, he lived his adult life in California where he worked as an actor in movies and television.
2. Between 1937 and the late 1950s he appeared in more than fifty movies.
3. His political persuasion changed from liberal to conservative as he grew older.
4. As President, he sought "peace through strength," increasing military spending by 35%.
5. He witnessed the end of the Cold War and the collapse of the Soviet Union.
6. Though his popularity rose and fell during his eight years as President, he retired in 1989 with an impressive approval rating above 60%.

Jimmy Carter
(1924-)
Thirty-ninth President (1977-81):
"We must adjust to changing times and still hold fast to unchanging principles."

1. Born and raised in Plains, Georgia, Carter graduated from the U. S. Naval Academy in Annapolis, Maryland and served seven years as an officer in the U. S. Navy.
2. A farmer, he entered Georgia state politics in 1962 and was elected Governor of his state in 1970.
3. As Governor, Carter began to deal with the results of generations of racism in Georgia.
4. He expanded the national park system to include more than 100 million acres of Alaskan wilderness.
5. He was the first President to urge conservation of oil and other non-renewable energy resources.
6. He protested the Soviet invasion of Afghanistan by refusing to allow American athletes to participate in the 1980 Olympics.

Gerald Ford
(1913-2006)
Thirty-eighth President (1974-1977):
"Truth is the glue that holds governments together."

1. Although born in Nebraska, he was a life-long citizen of Michigan.
2. He earned his law degree at Yale, where he also worked as a football coach to help pay his tuition.
3. Elected to the U.S. House of Representatives in 1948, he was still serving there when President Nixon chose him to be Vice President in 1973.
4. He is the only President never to have been elected either President or Vice President.
5. Respected by both Republicans and Democrats, he helped the United States recover from the Watergate scandal.
6. His wife, Betty, helped the nation learn to deal effectively with breast cancer and alcoholism, illnesses she suffered from.

George W. Bush
(1946-)
Forty-third President (2001-2009):
"If you don't feel something strongly you're not going to achieve."

1. He is a graduate of Yale University and of Harvard University's Business School.
2. He was a part-owner of the Texas Rangers baseball franchise.
3. He and his wife Laura have twin daughters, Barbara and Jenna, born in 1981.
4. Under his leadership, the United States has contributed heavily to the worldwide battle against HIV/AIDS.
5. President Bush enjoyed an increase in the annual presidential salary from $200,000 to $400,000.
6. During his presidency, America's national debt nearly doubled, rising to almost ten trillion dollars ($10,000,000,000,000).

Bill Clinton
(1946-)
Forty-second President (1993-2001):
"There is nothing wrong in America that can't be fixed with what is right in America."

1. President Clinton was born William Jefferson Blythe III but was adopted by his step-father, Roger Clinton.
2. He married Hillary Rodham in 1975. At the end of her eight years as First Lady, she was elected a senator from New York in 2000 and was a leading contender for the Democratic nomination for President in 2008.
3. Like President George H. W. Bush, he was highly skilled at building international alliances. He helped preserve the peace in such violent areas of the world as Bosnia.
4. Although impeached by a hostile Congress, he was not convicted by the Senate. He retired in 2001 with the highest approval rating of any President in the post-World War II era.
5. In retirement, President Clinton has done a lot of work to expand funding for HIV/AIDS research and treatment, especially in Africa.

George H. W. Bush
(1924-)
Forty-first President (1989-1993):
"I want a kinder, gentler nation."

1. Born into a wealthy and powerful family, President Bush volunteered for the army air force at the age of 18 and fought heroically in World War II.
2. After the war he enrolled as a student at Yale University where he was both a fine athlete and a member of the honorary academic society, Phi Beta Kappa.
3. He left the Connecticut of his youth and moved to Texas.
4. Bush served two terms as a member of the House of Representatives and then as the U. S. Ambassador to the UN.
5. In 1980 Ronald Reagan chose him as his vice presidential candidate.
6. He enjoyed a 90% approval rating after the Gulf War in 1991 but lost his bid for re-election in 1992.

The Oval Office
The Oval Office is 36 feet at its longest and 29 feet wide at its widest. The ceiling rises to an impressive height of 18.5 feet. The Oval Office has been the official place of business for U. S. Presidents since 1909.

1. President William Howard Taft had the first Oval Office built inside the newly-constructed West Wing in 1909. He had the walls covered with green grass-cloth.
2. President Hoover had the Office rebuilt in 1929, following a severe fire in the White House. In the 1930s, President Franklin Roosevelt completely redesigned the West Wing, and moved the Oval Office closer to the residential section of the White House.
3. The most famous piece of furniture is the Resolute desk, built from timbers salvaged from the British ship HMS Resolute and given to President Rutherford B. Hayes by Queen Victoria of England in 1880. Most Presidents since that time have used the desk.

The White House
The President's house at 1600 Pennsylvania Avenue is the most famous address in the United States, and among the best-known in the world.

1. Construction began in 1792, relying on crews of free men and slaves, and on November 1,1800, John Adams, the Second President, moved into the mansion for the final four months of his term. Mrs. Adams used the unfinished East Room to dry the family laundry.
2. The British burned the mansion in 1814, during the war of 1812, and rebuilding took from 1815 until 1817.
3. The first indoor bathroom was installed in 1833, gas lighting in 1848, and central heating in 1853. Electric lights appeared in 1891.
4. In 1909 the West Wing offices and the famous Oval Office were added. In 1927 an entire third floor was added to the mansion as more living space for the President and his family.
5. Although the White House has always been a tourist attraction, most Americans got to know the House best when Mrs. John F. Kennedy guided a televised tour through the building on February 14, 1962.

Barack Obama
(1961 -)
Forty-fourth President (2009 -):
"Change will not come if we wait for some other person or some other time. We are the ones we've been waiting for. We are the change that we seek."

1. He is the first African-American President, the son of a black man from Kenya and a white woman from Kansas.
2. His wife Michelle and he are graduates of Harvard University's School of Law.
3. After graduating from law school, he received nearly 650 job offers, but chose to work as a community organizer in Chicago rather than join a law firm.
4. The Obamas have two daughters, Malia and Natasha (Sasha).
5. His two books, *Dreams from My Father* and *The Audacity of Hope*, are best-sellers, earning him millions of dollars.
6. He won the Democratic nomination and the national election in no small part because of his insistence that the Iraq war was a huge mistake.